What Others Are Saying

This is one of those rare books that is easy to pick up and almost impossible to put down. Extremely practical and endlessly interesting, *Living for God* should be read by every Christian believer. Frank Hasel has made living for the glory of God as attractive as it should be. A truly outstanding book.

John Bradshaw, speaker/director, It Is Written

Frank Hasel has done something unique in *Living for God*. He has grounded all moral virtues in the love of God and removed from them any sense of meritorious burden. This is a deeply satisfying book for all those craving the joy of Christian virtue.

Ty Gibson, pastor and author

In this jewel of a book, Frank Hasel shows the beauty of Christian virtue from angle after alluring angle. As a Christian mental health counselor, I have witnessed firsthand how virtuous habits promote psychological flourishing and rich, true pleasure. May this book reset our love for God and His law!

Jennifer Jill Schwirzer, LPC, author, counselor, musician, speaker

Using personal stories, including the tragic loss of his own wife, Frank Hasel has written a readable, yet deep and moving book about virtue—a topic that, amid the cacophony of voices and current issues in both the world and the church, has almost been forgotten. After reading this great book, you won't think about Christian virtue the same. Nor should you.

Clifford Goldstein, director, Adult Sabbath School Bible Study Guides, General Conference of Seventh-day Adventists

Real, radical, and very relevant, *Living for God* is an inspiring and convicting call to virtuous living in an unvirtuous world. This book is a must-read for all those who long to be more like Jesus! I've been moved, convicted, and challenged through these pages. I know you will be too.

Melody Mason, author of the best-seller *Daring to Ask for More*

In reading Frank Hasel's book *Living for God*, I found myself craving virtue. Prepare to have your hunger for holiness both stimulated through reading and satisfied through Christ.

Doug Batchelor, president, Amazing Facts

In a world so bereft of morality, comes this gentle but bracing call to pursue what no one wants to talk about—virtue. Tapping our hunger for authenticity, humility, and even digital detox, Frank Hasel engages third millennial readers where we struggle most. He effectively shares through the prism of his own suffering and loss—where, as it turns out, the virtues of Jesus shine brightest. So be bold. And read on.

Dwight Nelson, senior pastor, Pioneer Memorial Church

One of my habits as a pastor is to share good books with the congregations I serve, including Frank Hasel's previous books. *Living for God* is well worth reading, and I look forward to enthusiastically sharing it with my church family!

Chad Stuart, senior pastor, Spencerville Seventh-day Adventist Church

Beautiful. Absolutely beautiful. Frank Hasel has drawn from his personal experience and deep understanding of God's Word to bring us into the presence of Jesus, where, by beholding Him, we become changed. *Living for God* enables us to reclaim the joy of virtue—the very essence of our Savior.

L. Ann Hamel, psychologist, Missionary Care Team,
General Conference of Seventh-day Adventists

Living for God describes the treasure of Biblical virtues in heartwarming and thought-provoking ways. It outlines some of the best character qualities of Frank's best friend, Jesus—providing practical tips for becoming more like Him. As one of Frank's colleagues, it's clear to me that he is not merely talking theory but sharing his own authentic journey to reclaim the joy of Christian virtue.

Janet Page, associate ministerial secretary,
General Conference of Seventh-day Adventists

Living for God is a timely book for a lukewarm church in a selfish and divided world. Based on his own encounter with his Savior and his experience as a committed disciple of Christ, Frank Hasel challenges and encourages his readers to follow the virtuous example of Jesus, who is the real and only remedy for sin and its devastating consequences.

Mario Brito, president, Inter-European Division of Seventh-day Adventists

Frank Hasel positions virtue as essential to living for God. While typical definitions of *virtue* highlight moral and ethical faithfulness, this book demonstrates that virtuous living is even more valuable—empowering us to exemplify Christ's love in all aspects of life. With sound biblical wisdom and testimonies of victorious living, this book will provide valuable guidance and practical encouragement to its many readers.

Ella Simmons, general vice president,
General Conference of Seventh-day Adventists

I have been deeply impressed and blessed by *Living for God*'s in-depth elaboration of Christian virtue. The book shares many practical tools for developing the virtues God created us to enjoy. This is a must-read for all who wish to experience the joy of Christian virtue.

Si Young Kim, president, Northern Asia-Pacific Division of Seventh-day Adventists

Living for God is a breath of fresh air: practical, relevant, encouraging. Frank Hasel offers a rare perspective on the Christian journey, with biblical keys to help grow your life in Christ. This book inspired me to be all that He has called me to be. I cried. I was convicted yet comforted. If you are serious about your walk with Jesus, this book is for you!

Jill Morikone, vice president/COO, Three Angels Broadcasting Network

This is one of the best books ever on practical Christian living. It puts everything into perspective and shows in practical terms what Christ's fathomless love, His righteousness, and His perfect example actually mean in our daily Christian experience—the beauty of how Christ works in and through us to transform us into His likeness, ultimately fulfilling all the desires of our hearts.

Nancy Wilson, wife of General Conference President Ted N. C. Wilson

LIVING FOR
GOD

RECLAIMING THE JOY OF CHRISTIAN VIRTUE

FRANK M. HASEL

Pacific Press®
Publishing Association
Nampa, Idaho | www.pacificpress.com

Cover design by Steve Lanto
Cover design resources from iStockphoto.com | 615521268
Inside design by Aaron Troia

The author assumes full responsibility for the accuracy of all facts and quotations as cited in this book.

Additional copies of this book may be purchased by calling toll-free 1-800-765-6955 or by visiting AdventistBookCenter.com.

ISBN 978-0-8163-6620-0

January 2020

Dedication

To
my mother

Berbel Hasel
(December 10, 1933–November 8, 2019)

who exemplified love and dedication and excelled in
living a virtuous life in rather challenging circumstances.

You were
a virtuous woman
and a true
hero of my heart!

Also by Frank M. Hasel

Adventists and Military Service: Biblical, Historical, and Ethical Perspectives (coedited with Barna Magyarosi and Stefan Höschele)

How to Interpret Scripture (coauthored with Michael G. Hasel)

Longing for God: A Prayer and Bible Journal

Table of Contents

Acknowledgments

Living a virtuous life is something that requires lifelong learning. This book has grown out of my journey so far. The best journeys are not made in isolation but in the company of good friends. I have been privileged to enjoy the friendship of some special people whom I would like to recognize and affirm.

My General Conference friends—I have been so blessed by your support. We have shared lunch in the cafeteria, laughter, prayers, and many meaningful conversations. I have been enriched by your wisdom and diversity, challenged by your questions, inspired by your creativity and passion, and touched by your kindness. What a joy it has been to explore new insights into the beauty and mystery of life with you. I will be eternally grateful for those meaningful moments, and for the inspiration I have drawn from them.

This book would not have seen the light of day without the help and support of numerous people who gently nudged me to sit down and actually start writing despite my busy schedule. Their encouragement and constructive criticism turned out to be an enormous help in many ways. The feedback I received from them made the first draft even better. Thank you to all those who believed in this book and helped it succeed.

Elise Harboldt—Thank you for your attentive interest in this book. Your feedback and edits significantly improved its readability.

You truly have a rare gift of expressing complex ideas in positive and engaging ways that help people to think creatively and deeply about God's love. You have an astute ability to reason theologically and a passion for reaching those who are put off by shallow, mediocre thinking, or the meaningless repetition of pious language. May we all experience fascination and awe again when we talk and think of God. You have succeeded in doing just that. Thank you for your deep desire to express God's life-changing love in more meaningful ways.

Melody Mason—A heartfelt thank you for your feedback about the initial title of the book. You triggered a creative process that led to the current title, which seems like a much better fit.

Pacific Press friends—Many thanks to Scott Cady and Dale Galusha, who first approached me with the idea of writing a sequel to my first best-selling book with Pacific Press, *Longing for God*. Your continued interest and support in the project is very much appreciated.

Jutta Sikora and family—In order to meet the book's deadline, I needed to write it during my annual vacation while visiting relatives in Germany and Austria. A special "thank you" to my sister Jutta and her family for being such generous hosts for many weeks. You provided the perfect setting at your beautiful home. It was just the right environment to allow quiet and undisturbed time, encouraging the flow of my thoughts and words. Without that peaceful setting, I'm afraid the book would still be unfinished.

My mother, Berbel Hasel—Her prayers were a constant source of blessing, and her genuine interest in my personal well-being was such an encouragement to me. Shortly before the book was finished, my mother died. It is with great gratitude for her tender love and for her inspiring example of genuine kindness in the midst of rather challenging circumstances that I dedicate this book to her.

My sons—A special thanks to Jonathan, Florian, and Daniel. It was fun and rewarding to share some of my ideas with you and to brainstorm ways of making the book more appealing for a wider audience. I learn so much from your expertise in a wide variety of areas. Being your dad has taught me many valuable lessons about virtuous living. I am humbly proud of each one of you and find joy watching you master your lives in many ways. Let's see what can grow out of our dreams and humble beginnings. Most important, let's determine, no matter what, to be men of virtue in whom God delights.

Ellen G. White (1827–1915)—She was an American Christian pioneer, activist, abolitionist, health reformer, and author—the most broadly translated female author (of non-fiction) in the history of literature. She was named one of the top one hundred most influential Americans of all time by *Smithsonian Magazine*.* She wrote on a wide variety of subjects, including biblical theology, social justice, health, nutrition, education, psychology, interpersonal relationships, agriculture, and more. Ellen White was instrumental in establishing multiple schools and medical centers around the world, such as Loma Linda University Medical Center in California. Because I have found her writings to be remarkably helpful and inspiring, I have included several quotations from her throughout the book. To learn more about this influential woman, visit ellengwhitetruth.com.

---

* T.A. Frail, "The 100 Most Significant Americans of All Time," *Smithsonian Magazine*, November 17, 2014, https://www.smithsonianmag.com/smithsonianmag/meet-100-most-significant-americans-all-time-180953341/?no-ist

Introduction

The precepts of the LORD are right, giving joy to the heart . . .
in keeping them there is great reward.

—Psalm 19:8, 11, NIV

Do you know what you crave? Deep down inside, do you actually know what it is you most desire? If you're like most human beings, you sometimes get confused about your cravings.

People speak of craving chocolate, potato chips, and other edible temptations. But has anyone ever told you they're craving virtue? Probably not. A virtue can be defined as a quality of moral excellence or goodness. We often assume that morality fights *against* our cravings. But I'm convinced that virtuous living actually satisfies us in ways nothing else can. It is a distinction that gives our lives special worth.

Whether we know it or not, we deeply crave the pleasure and quality of virtue, because we're made in the image of Love. Sin and selfishness always cause harm and emptiness, not only to those we hurt but to our own well-being. We are designed to live lives of virtue.

Describing the human longing, King Solomon wrote, "What a person desires is unfailing love" (Proverbs 19:22, NIV). We also know from Scripture that love awakens love in the hearts of those who experience it: "We love because he first loved us" (1 John 4:19, NIV).

As human beings, we find our ultimate joy in giving and receiving love. But what does this mean, practically speaking, and how can we build it into our day-to-day lives? My book *Longing for God* describes practical ways to *experience* God's love through engaging with Scripture and prayer. This book shares lessons on *living out* that love through a lifestyle of virtue.

Being a virtuous person is a process that lasts a lifetime. Virtuous living is not merely a mental disposition to behave properly or act nobly. It goes much deeper than that, touching and healing our attitudes, motives, beliefs, and actions. This process leads to an experience of increasing freedom and faithfulness.

Virtuous living is as broad as it is beautiful. It encompasses, among other things, such qualities as *attentiveness* to what others have to say, *fair-mindedness* in our interactions, *honesty* in our search for truth, and *open-mindedness* to learning new things. Virtuous living means *carefulness* in what we speak and do, *courage* to tackle the unfamiliar, *friendliness* toward those whom we come in contact with, and *resilience and hope* in times of trouble. True virtuous living does not grow in times of leisure when life is going smoothly. The virtuous character is formed in times of pressure when we are tempted to compromise truth, or our faith is put to the test.

Put simply, a virtuous life is a life of practical and comprehensive *love*. Virtues shape how we live our lives through integrity and love. They express the very best we can be in God's sight. We see these virtues perfectly embodied in the life of Jesus Christ. He is our inspiration and example of what it means to live a virtuous life.

The lessons in this little book have grown out of my own encounter with my Savior and His written Word.* Where appropriate, I have shared some of my personal experiences. I still have much room to grow, but I have discovered that when I live out God's virtues, they bring me peace and joy. I have also included some stories from other people's lives.

---

* I have shared some of my ideas previously, in sermons and in articles in various publications. They have matured and are further developed in this book. Learning is a lifelong activity.

As you practice virtuous living, you will experience life more meaningfully, adding a depth and quality that you didn't know before. Virtue is a true blessing, bringing joy to God, others, and ourselves. Virtues enlarge the quality of our relationships and elevate the level of our social abilities. But they are more than just markers of interpersonal excellence. Ultimately, virtues are living expressions of God's character. When manifested in our lives, they bring healing to others and glory to Him.

You don't have to be a hero to live virtuously. But if you, through the power of the Holy Spirit, develop a virtuous lifestyle in all its practical dimensions, you will be a true hero of God's heart. May you be inspired to live a virtuous life for the glory of God, the blessing of others, and the fulfillment of your deepest longings, because "His divine power has granted to us all things that pertain to life and godliness, through the knowledge of him who called us to his own glory and excellence. . . . For this very reason, make every effort to supplement your faith with virtue, and virtue with knowledge" (2 Peter 1:3–5, ESV).

Chapter 1

Virtuous Hearts and Minds

Intelligence plus character—that is the goal of true education.
—Martin Luther King Jr.

"I love you with all of my mind!"

Have you ever heard this expression in a romantic film, or included in someone's wedding vows? Probably not. This expression of love sounds foreign at first, not nearly as genuine or affectionate as the traditional, "I love you with all my heart." But there's something uniquely special about being loved by someone's mind. It's a beautiful thing when a person stretches their mental capacities in order to understand and love more intelligently.

The more we know God, the more we will love Him and others. We can express our love through *words* as we "[speak] the truth in love" (Ephesians 4:15). We can express our love in *actions* by being "rich in good works, ready to give, willing to share" (1 Timothy 6:18). We can also express our love in a way that's often overlooked: by loving with our *minds*.

We typically think of love primarily as an emotion. God *does* want His love to touch our hearts and influence our feelings. But He *also* wants it to touch our minds and influence our thoughts.

The New Testament records an important conversation between Jesus and a lawyer. This conversation deals with matters of eternal consequence. He asked Jesus what it takes to inherit eternal life. Jesus asked the man to recall what Scripture says. He responded, " 'You shall *love the Lord your God* with all your heart, with all your soul, with all your strength, and with *all your mind,*' and 'your neighbor as yourself' " (Luke 10:27; emphasis added). Jesus approved of this answer.

This is a remarkable statement. You shall *love* God, not just with your heart, but *with all your mind*! The Greek word used for "mind" here is διάνοια (*dianoia*), which describes the "activity of thinking," "comprehending," "reasoning," and "reflecting" in the sense of understanding something.[1] As the crowning work of God's creation, we have been given the gift of intelligent thought—the capacity to reflect on life, God, nature, science, other people, and ourselves.

Psychologists estimate that human minds think between sixty thousand and eighty thousand thoughts per day. That's about three thousand thoughts per hour! Our thoughts are precious resources that can be used to improve our lives and the lives of those around us. Right thinking can also bring joy to the Creator of our minds: "Behold, You desire truth in the inward parts, and in the hidden part You will make me to know wisdom" (Psalm 51:6).

Virtuous thinking honors God and helps us develop into all we can be.[2] Let's look at some of the key characteristics of virtuous thinking: intellectual carefulness, intellectual fair-mindedness, intellectual honesty, and intellectual humility.

Intellectual carefulness

Whenever we are trying to understand something, whether its another person's behavior, a complex situation, or knowledge about any topic of interest, we need to cultivate intellectual carefulness.

People who are intellectually careful want to sincerely know the truth. They refuse to rush to hasty conclusions based on limited knowledge.[3] Instead, they are thorough and diligent in their thinking and decision-making, cautious not to overlook important details.

We all know of cases in which careless thinking in work, studies, relationships, science, and theology has led to disastrous results. Sometimes these negative results are seen quickly. Other times, they become evident later. But careless thinking is always dangerous.

A tragic example of intellectual carelessness can be seen in the fateful crashes of two Boeing 737 MAX airplanes—one crash off the Indonesian coast in 2018, and the other in Ethiopia just five months later. These crashes killed 346 people. A faulty software system was implicated. This software had a critical flaw, which caused the planes to unexpectedly and repeatedly nosedive. The Federal Aviation Administration's regulatory process gave Boeing significant oversight authority, and this contributed to the compromised safety of the Boeing 737 MAX airplanes.[4] Careless thinking led to the tragic deaths of hundreds of precious people. It also led to significant embarrassment and financial loss for Boeing and the Federal Aviation Administration.

The example of Jesus compels us to think and work carefully. His carefulness, displayed in creation and seen throughout His life on earth, should inspire our carefulness in thinking. God is never in a hurry, but He is always on time. We do not honor Him when we are not careful and thorough in what we think, believe, say, plan, and do. Intellectual carefulness will lead to success in every area of life. Put positively, you can love God with all your heart *and mind* by being intellectually careful!

Intellectual fair-mindedness
We live in a world of bias. Turn on the news, and you're likely to hear current events explained in a partisan and polemic way. This spirit of bias can seep into our thinking in ways we don't even realize. Many people have strong opinions on politics, ethics, theology, lifestyle, and, well . . . essentially everything. But few people are willing to carefully and impartially consider thoughts and ideas that might challenge their own biases.

Fair-minded people earnestly want to know the truth and therefore are willing to listen to different opinions in an objective and unbiased way.[5] It's impossible to be fair-minded if we think we already know everything and already possess all truth. On the other hand, if we start to believe that truth is relative and that every viewpoint is equally important, the virtue of fair-mindedness will morph into meaninglessness, and the end of education will not be far.[6] We want to be open-minded but "not so open-minded that our brains fall out!"[7]

Fair-mindedness does not mean that we have no convictions or that we won't stand for our convictions. The secret of fair-minded people is that they have chosen to put the truth over any allegiance to their egos or cherished opinions. Therefore, fair-minded people are consistently willing to listen in an even-handed way to different opinions, even if they already have a strong view on the subject. Fair-minded people also try to view issues from the perspectives of those they disagree with because they are aware that they do not always have the most complete or accurate perspective on a given topic. An intellectually fair-minded person cares more about knowing what's actually true than about convincing themselves or others that they are right. Intellectual bias is the corresponding vice.[8]

Let's explore just a few of the many advantages of fair-minded thinking. First, the fair-minded person is able to escape from a prison of false assumptions. The following historical anecdote illustrates the point.

In seventeenth-century Europe, the astronomer Johannes Kepler committed himself to a greater understanding of the stars and planets. Because of Aristotle, the Western world had firmly assumed that the universe revolved around the earth. Being so convinced, the Catholic Church had interpreted key passages of Scripture in line with Aristotelian logic, which had proven reliable in many other areas. Not only had significant church doctrine been built around this theory, but scientific inquiry had also been rooted in the same set of assumptions.

This perspective was so pervasive that people failed to challenge their assumptions. Those who noticed inconsistencies between the popular view and the way the universe actually behaved, simply created increasingly extravagant explanations as to why these inconsistencies were actually in harmony with the commonly held view.

What distinguished Kepler from his predecessors (beyond accumulating evidence that undermined the accepted view) was his willingness to look at the evidence in a genuinely fair-minded way. It is unlikely that Kepler was any more intelligent than his educated predecessors and peers. He was, however, willing to objectively and impartially consider other possible explanations for the evidence. Kepler's contribution eventually transformed our understanding of the universe and led to a host of other innovations that form the foundation of science today.[9]

But fair-mindedness isn't just for nerds or academics. This way of thinking also has practical relational benefits. Genuinely fair-minded people tend to make and keep friends more easily than those whose thinking habits are closed-minded or biased. Why? The reason is simple. There is an inherent link between fair-mindedness and attentive listening. Because they are committed to discovering truth, fair-minded people actually listen! Active listening helps people feel genuinely valued and respected.

Fair-minded people are curious learners, active listeners, and brave explorers of truth. This habit adds invaluable depth, richness, and wisdom to life. Put positively, you can love God with all your heart *and mind* when you are intellectually fair-minded.

Intellectual honesty

You likely have heard the old adage, "Honesty is the best policy." Of all the intellectual virtues, honesty is perhaps the most admired, but the least practiced. Unlike other intellectual character traits, intellectual honesty is not primarily about the process of *getting* knowledge but rather about how we choose to *use* or *present* the knowledge we already have. The intellectually honest person won't use information out of context, exaggerate facts, distort the truth by describing it with loaded language, or mislead others by using statistics or any other type of supporting evidence that might have a deceptive effect. In addition, intellectually honest people do not take credit for ideas that are not their own.[10]

The casualty of honesty is perhaps best illustrated by the fact that in 2017 the *Collins English Dictionary* chose *fake news* as the word of the year. It defines it as "false, often sensational, information disseminated under the guise of news reporting."[11] Today this practice is so common that people have almost grown to expect it.

Using or manipulating knowledge in a dishonest way causes a battle with the conscience. Unless the conscience wins, one of two negative outcomes will occur. The first possible outcome is a life weighed down with a heavy load of guilt. While intellectual honesty may seem to be a difficult road, in the end, it's characterized by much greater freedom.[12] The second outcome is even worse. Intellectual dishonesty can lead to the death of the conscience, endangering moral integrity. When we distort the truth and then create a moral code that justifies our actions, the result is a corrupted intellectual conscience that no longer values the truth. A dishonest person will eventually have difficulty altogether distinguishing truth from falsehood![13] The dangerous thing about dishonesty is that, in the end, you firmly believe your own lie.[14]

On the other hand, honesty builds internal self-respect and relational trust. This trust is at the core of all healthy relationships and communities. It is essential for God's people to practice honesty in order to reflect His love and win the confidence of those we wish to reach. Put positively, you can love God with all your heart *and mind* when you practice intellectual honesty!

Intellectual humility

The virtue of intellectual humility is perhaps the most misunderstood virtue. So what does it mean to be humble in the way we think?

Intellectually humble people have the amazing realization and humbling insight that they are dependent upon something or someone outside themselves. They are aware that truth is not of their own making but is ultimately God-breathed. Realizing that their reason and rational intelligence is not the measure of everything,[15] they gladly submit their thoughts to God in obedience to Christ and His Word (2 Corinthians 10:5).

Intellectually humble people understand that the larger their egos the less space in their minds for anything or anyone else. Humility of thought has countless benefits. Humble curiosity is the foundation of all growth in knowledge. It naturally produces a teachable spirit, making humble people very pleasant to work with.

Intellectual humility does not lead to a lack of firm conviction. Humble Christians are confident in God's truth and submissive to it. At the same time, they are aware of the limitations of their own knowledge. Therefore, they are capable of expanding their understanding of the world in a way that arrogant and proud people are utterly incapable of.[16] Proud people don't feel the need to learn from anyone but think they know all there is to know. If we want to continue to learn and grow, our knowledge must be tempered by humility.[17]

President Abraham Lincoln modeled intellectual humility in a remarkable way.[18] At the height of the American Civil War, Lincoln was doing everything in his power to preserve the unity of his crumbling country. As the nation's elected president and one of the most intelligent men of his generation, Lincoln had every right to expect deferential respect from his subordinates. And yet, as the war waged, he found himself criticized and ridiculed by friends and foes alike. One whom Lincoln initially considered a friend was his secretary of war, Edwin Stanton. Both publicly and privately, Stanton made no secret of his disdain for Lincoln. Even though Lincoln was aware of Stanton's insubordination, he kept him as secretary of war, believing that Stanton's sharp mind and independent perspective would be a valuable balance to his own.

At one of the war's most critical points, Lincoln sent a direct order to Stanton. Not only did Stanton refuse to carry it out, but he also called Lincoln a fool. Instead of reacting in anger or spite, Lincoln responded, " 'If Stanton said I was a . . . fool, then I must be one. For he is nearly always right, and generally says what he means. I will step over and see him.' "[19]

Lincoln was no weakling. He had demonstrated many times that he was willing to stand his ground if necessary. Still, as the story goes, the two men had a meeting in which Lincoln listened carefully to his subordinate, concluded that Stanton was right after all, and withdrew his order. Lincoln ignored the demands of pride in order to pursue the wisest course. Ultimately, this intellectual humility helped save his crumbling nation and ensured his reputation as one of the greatest statesmen in the history of the United States of America.

Put positively, you can love God with all your heart *and mind* when you are intellectually humble.

As followers of Christ, we can love God with all our hearts *and minds* by being intellectually careful, fair-minded, honest, and humble. In addition to the benefits already described, these intellectual virtues also enhance our ability to worship God. Entering into meaningful worship is closely tied to the character of our minds.

As we apply our minds to understand God through His written Word and created works, our ability to worship Him increases. While worship includes far more than an intellectual understanding of God, this understanding is still important. Our worship and relationship with God depend on the full engagement of our minds. You cannot truly worship God without thinking.

How we think also influences how we behave. When we practice the habits of virtuous thinking, our actions will reflect God's goodness. When we are careful in what we say about others, treat their opinions in a fair-minded way, are honest in our dealings, and cultivate curiosity and humility, we allow God to reveal His gracious love through us![20] This is how God deals with each one of us.

Imagine if our homes, places of work, churches, schools, and communities were filled with people of such character and attitude. What a fellowship that would be! Imagine how the relationships and the atmosphere within the home, the church, and the world at large would change for the better if we all practiced virtuous thinking. God would be delighted, people would be attracted, and each one of us would be greatly blessed! May you experience the joy of loving God and others with all your heart *and mind* by choosing the freedom of virtuous thinking.

God be in my head, and in my thinking.
God be in my eyes, and in my looking.
God be in my mouth, and in my speaking.
Oh, God be in my heart, and in my understanding.[21]

Reflection questions
1. How does your love for God influence your ability to think and reflect?
2. Reflect on a time when you had the opportunity to exercise each of the four virtues mentioned. What happened?
3. How can you listen more attentively to the people around you?
4. Experiment with attentive listening and make a list of the benefits.
5. The biggest fake news of all time is that God is *not* love. How does rejecting that fake news help us to live the virtuous life?
6. In what way does living the virtuous life help us to love God and worship Him better?

1. See "διάνοια, ας, ἡ" in William Arndt Frederick W. Danker, Walter Bauer, and F. Wilbur Gingrich, *A Greek-English Lexicon of the New Testament and Other Early Christian Literature* (Chicago, IL: University of Chicago Press, 2000), 234.

2. Philip E. Dow, *Virtuous Minds: Intellectual Character Development* (Downers Grove, IL: InterVarsity, 2013).

3. Cf. Dow, *Virtuous Minds,* 147.

4. Michael Barbaro, "The Origins of Boeing's 737 Max Crisis," July 30, 2019, in *The Daily,* produced by Michael Simon Johnson, Jessica Cheung, Clare Toeniskoetter, podcast, MP3 audio, 26 :16, accessed, August 30, 2019, https://www.nytimes.com/2019/07/30 /podcasts/the-daily/boeing-737-max.html?searchResultPosition=2. See also Anurag Kotoky and Kyunghee Park, "When Will Boeing 737 Max Fly Again and More Questions," *The Washington Post,* August 18, 2019, accessed August 30, 2019, https://www.washingtonpost.com /business/when-will-boeing-737-max-fly-again-and-more-questions/2019/08/15/5ae3096c -ee1d-11e9-bb7e-d2026ee0c199_story.html.

5. Dow, *Virtuous Minds,* 149.

6. Dow, *Virtuous Minds,* 48. For a powerful argument in favor of truth, see Princeton professor Harry G. Frankfort's short book *On Truth* (New York: Alfred E. Knopf, 2006).

7. Walter Kotschnig, speech given at Mount Holyoke College in Massachusetts, January 27, 1940, "Professor Tells Students to Open Minds to Truth," *Blytheville Courier News,* Quote Page 2, Column 2 and 3, Blytheville, AR (NewspaperArchive), cited in Quote Investigator, accessed November 10, 2019, https://quoteinvestigator.com/tag/walter-kotschnig/.

8. Cf. Dow, *Virtuous Minds,* 49, 149.

9. Dow, *Virtuous Minds,* 51–53.

10. Dow, *Virtuous Minds,* 61–69, 151. I honestly admit my great indebtedness to the ideas in Dow's remarkable book.

11. *Collins* online dictionary, s.v. "fake news," accessed August 23, 2019, https://www .collinsdictionary.com/word-lovers-blog/new/collins-2017-word-of-the-year-shortlist ,396,HCB.html.

12. Dow, *Virtuous Minds,* 66.

13. Dow, *Virtuous Minds,* 66.

14. Robert Spaemann, *Gut und Böse—relativ? Über die Allgemeingültigkeit sittlicher Normen* (Freiburg: Herder Verlag, 1996), 13, 14, points out that human language is the medium to express our thoughts and that lying makes the real thoughts of a person invisible and thus leads to a disappearing of the person because the medium of language that makes the person visible is destroyed.

15. Cf. Dow, *Virtuous Minds,* 72, 152, 153.

16. Cf. Dow, *Virtuous Minds,* 72.

17. Kevin J. Vanhoozer, *Is There a Meaning in This Text? The Bible, the Reader, and the Morality of Literary Knowledge* (Grand Rapids, MI: Zondervan, 1998), 462.

18. See Dow, *Virtuous Minds,* 72, 73.

19. Carl Sandburg, *Abraham Lincoln: The Prairie Years and the War Years* (New York: Mariner, 2002), 354, as quoted in Dow, *Virtuous Minds,* 196.

20. Cf. Dow, *Virtuous Minds,* 97, 98.

21. *Sarum Primer* (1558), as quoted in "God Be In My Head," *The Seventh-day Adventist Hymnal* (Washington, DC: Review and Herald®, 1991), no. 679. The text has been beautifully put to music by John Rutter and the Cambridge Singers on YouTube, accessed November 10, 2019, https://www.youtube.com/watch?v=yGMcFt61yjo.

Chapter 2

A Virtuous Legacy

Character may be manifested in the great moments,
but it is made in the small ones.

—Phillips Brooks

I would like to ask you a challenging yet very significant question. If you could choose just two qualities that you would like to be remembered for at the end of your life, two words that would depict what you stood for and valued the most, what two words would you choose?

Several years ago, while driving to the airport in Munich, Germany, I noticed billboards along the roadside that pictured a long, dark limousine with several people from show business. The heading said something about "the rich and the famous." The ad was an invitation to meet some of the most wealthy and famous people in Germany.

Many people today want to be "rich and famous." Of course, we know this will never bring lasting joy or satisfaction. The most important things in life—love, hope, trust, friendship, happiness, health—cannot be bought!

But even those of us who don't dream of riches or fame have a tendency to strive for recognition. We want to be known as successful, smart, attractive, popular, competent, and so on.

Deep down, human beings crave love and acceptance. God designed us this way. But we often get confused about how to receive this love and end up damaging ourselves in our efforts to obtain it.

This problem isn't new. Long ago, the prophet Jeremiah delivered a special message from God to the children of Israel. This is what God said, "For My people have committed two evils: They have forsaken Me, the fountain of living waters, and hewn themselves cisterns— broken cisterns that can hold no water" (Jeremiah 2:13).

The children of Israel desperately needed God's presence, His love, and His acceptance, which are represented by living water. But instead, they ended up thirsty and discontent after trying to have their needs met in other ways.

Our attempts to earn love and approval through pride, wealth, popularity, success, and other human measures are like "broken cisterns" that leave us thirsty and dry. But Jesus offers us something much better.

Shortly before His death, Jesus desperately wanted people to understand the value of what He had to give. On the last day of the Passover, He stood up and loudly called out, "If anyone thirsts, let him come to Me and drink. He who believes in Me, as the Scripture has said, out of his heart will flow rivers of living water" (John 7:37, 38).

The sweet promise of the gospel is a twofold, or "double," promise. In addition to satisfying *our* thirst, Jesus also promises to make us channels of living water to others. This double blessing is exactly what human beings most crave. In the words of psychiatrist David Viscott, "To love and be loved is to feel the sun from both sides."[1]

Christian virtues are like living water, flowing out of us as God's love flows in. With this in mind, I would like to explore a few of the virtues that bring lasting joy: faithfulness, kindness, and courage. These are excellent qualities for a Christian to practice and to be remembered by.

Faithfulness

Faithfulness is not as flashy as money or fame, but it is more essential and far more important to God. The wise King Solomon wrote,

Let not steadfast love and faithfulness forsake you;
  bind them around your neck;
  write them on the tablet of your heart.
So you will find favor and good success
  in the sight of God and man" (Proverbs 3:3, 4, ESV).

There is something peculiar about faithfulness. Though you can be a little bit famous or a little bit rich, you cannot be a little bit faithful. Faithfulness has something exclusive about it that demands undivided attention. Either you are faithful 100 percent or you are unfaithful. If you are faithful 95 percent, you are not faithful but unfaithful. Faithfulness requires total commitment. God wants your full, complete dedication. Let us be men and women who are faithful.

In the Old Testament, we read the story of Daniel, who was thrown into the lions' den because he was not willing to compromise his faith in God. When Daniel distinguished himself as a wise, dependable leader for the king, his enemies became envious and looked for ways to accuse him of wrongdoing. "But they could find no ground of accusation or evidence of corruption, inasmuch as he was faithful" (Daniel 6:4, NASB). My hope is that our enemies (if we have any) and our friends will discover the same about us! May we be people who are known and respected for our faithfulness in the daily things we do. Like Daniel, may we trust God to take care of us as we are faithful to His will.

I can testify from my own life and from the experience of my family that God delights in and honors faithfulness. My grandfather, Franz Hasel, was an ordained Seventh-day Adventist minister in Germany. Against his will, he was drafted into the army during World War II. Because my grandfather wanted to honor God's commandments, including "thou shalt not kill," he requested to serve in the medical corps and refused to use a weapon. But his request was not granted. Instead, he was placed into another unit as a unit clerk on the front lines. He took his conviction not to kill so seriously that he carried a wooden gun in his holster for the duration of the war. Although he thought he might die many times, God miraculously protected my grandfather time and time again. His inspiring story can be read in the book *A Thousand Shall Fall.*[2]

Faithfulness to God leads to lasting joy and satisfaction. It brings peace of mind because you know that what you are doing is pleasing to God and beneficial to those around you. Being faithful to the spouse you will marry or have married will protect your marriage and guard your love for each other. This faithfulness will be a tremendous blessing, not only to you but also to your family and to society at large. Faithfulness is like gold. It shines!

Nevertheless, you cannot be truly faithful without love—the ultimate foundation of all faithfulness. Without love, faithfulness morphs into legalism and mere duty, and eventually deteriorates into fanaticism.

During Hitler's regime, his elite soldiers, the infamous Schutzstaffel (more commonly referred to as SS), had a motto that every SS soldier wore on his belt. This motto stated, "Our honor is loyalty." This loyalty was blind "faithfulness" to the Führer and was nothing but fanaticism with disastrous results. This organization was perhaps the most responsible for committing the genocidal killing of the Jews, as well as multiple other war atrocities.

True faithfulness, in contrast, is motivated and carried out by love! This love for God and the well-being of humanity is coupled with persistence and endurance. A faithful person does not quit easily. A faithful person is diligent and reliable in the work he or she pursues. A faithful person perseveres. Such people can be trusted. Such faithfulness becomes visible in our loyalty to God, in our attention to the details of life, and in our love for others. It shows!

Faithfulness shows its beauty in the challenges of life. Our lives rarely run smoothly. There are difficulties to master and obstacles to overcome. There are attractions and distractions that vie for our attention and compete for our loyalty and devotion. This is the very context in which faithfulness grows and shows.

God never promised to deliver us from every difficulty or evil, but He *did* promise to be with us each step of the way. God did not deliver Daniel from being thrown into the lions' den, but He was *with* Daniel in the lions' den.[3] God is faithful. His love never changes. As the prophet Jeremiah has stated so beautifully, "Because of the LORD's great love we are not consumed, for his compassions never fail. They are new every morning; great is your faithfulness" (Lamentations 3:22, 23, NIV).

God's faithfulness is great, and so is His kindness. As we reflect God's image, our faithfulness is accompanied by genuine, *loving-kindness* and service to others. Let's explore this further.

Kindness

Loving-kindness is a universal language. It can be understood even by the deaf and seen even by the blind. When my youngest son, Daniel, was a child, he played with his friends at Bogenhofen[4] in Austria, where I was a teacher in the theology department. I also taught religion classes for international language students who wanted to learn or improve their German. Daniel's friends came from a wide variety of countries and spoke many different languages—Portuguese, French, Russian, English, German, to name but a few.

One day, a mother who spoke several languages fluently introduced her children to little Daniel and then asked him, "Daniel, do you speak French?"

Daniel shook his head.

"Do you speak Italian?"

Daniel shook his head.

"Do you speak English?"

Again, Daniel shook his head.

Then, as if she wanted to build a bridge for Daniel, she asked him in German (his mother tongue), "Do you speak German?"

"No!" Daniel responded.

By this time, the lady seemed a bit confused and flabbergasted. "Well, Daniel, what language *do* you speak?" she asked.

"I speak friendly!" Daniel responded.

There is no language barrier for friendliness. A friendly smile, a helping hand, support in times of need, and words of encouragement all go a long way to make life easier and much more pleasant. Let us be people who are known for our loving-kindness.

Shortly before His betrayal and death, after washing His disciples' feet, Jesus told them, "By this all will know that you are My disciples, if you have love for one another" (John 13:35).

Jesus knew that the kindness of His followers would be a powerful testimony of their faith. Echoing this idea, Ellen White wrote, "The strongest argument in favor of the gospel is a loving and lovable Christian."[5]

Through compassion for others, love can reach hearts beyond the borders of religion, race, wealth, and rank. God created every heart to respond to loving-kindness.

My grandfather, who I mentioned earlier, often told a story that is not included in *A Thousand Shall Fall*. While serving in Russia, far from home, his unit was assigned to search through the houses of every village that the Germans had captured on their advance into Russia. They were ordered to search for resistance fighters, who would hide inside homes and attack the advancing German troops. They were told to immediately and indiscriminately shoot every person they found hiding.

One day, as my grandfather was carefully searching a house, he had a feeling that something was unusual. When he entered a particular room, he found it empty, but still had an impression that something was suspicious. When he looked under the bed, he saw a young man staring right at him. My grandfather knew that if he exposed this young man, he would definitely be shot. They locked eyes for a split second that seemed like an eternity. Then my grandfather got up, left the room, and did not report what he had seen. He had pity on this young man.

Several weeks later, my grandfather was assigned to patrol an important railway track. His duty was to make sure that no resistance fighters bombed the tracks. He was watching alone when a group of Russian Cossacks rapidly charged at him on their horses. There was no way to escape. He braced himself for death, believing they would surely kill him.

The group quickly encircled him, but my grandfather was shocked when he saw the face of their leading commander. It was the same young man he had seen hiding under the bed in that house. They immediately recognized each other. The young Cossack commander pointed his gun at my grandfather and signaled to him, "I could kill you now," he indicated, "but you were kind enough to save my life. So I will spare your life!" Then he ordered his men to ride on. In God's providence, the life of my grandfather was spared. His loving-kindness returned to him.

God has given us the beautiful privilege of reflecting His faithfulness and kindness to others. Your loving acts of kindness can bring comfort and joy to both heaven and earth.

Courage

Faithfulness and loving-kindness go hand in hand with a third virtue: courage. This virtue is urgently needed in times of crisis, particularly in light of the significant challenges before us. Courage is something that God desires.

We need to learn to be tenacious people who will courageously move forward in difficult circumstances. Courageous people trust God and His promises in times of perplexity and trouble, refusing to be timid or despondent.

Courage is contagious. Our world desperately needs men and women who will resist the temptation to cower in the face of crisis but will instead move forward with courage and faith.

You do not need to have great faith, but you need to have faith in a great God. He will not leave you alone but has promised to help you in every difficulty.

One of the last chapters of the Bible reveals just how dangerous fear and distrust can be. Speaking of the contrast between believers and unbelievers, the apostle John wrote, "He who overcomes shall inherit all things, and I will be his God and he shall be My son. But the *cowardly,* unbelieving, abominable, murderers, sexually immoral, sorcerers, idolaters, and all liars shall have their part in the lake which burns with fire and brimstone, which is the second death" (Revelation 21:7, 8; emphasis added).

Most Christians easily recognize that the sins of murder, immorality, and idolatry are dangerous. But Scripture includes the cowardly in the group of people who do not inherit eternal life. It even lists them first. Why? Because cowardice is incompatible with faith. In order to truly believe in Jesus, we must believe that He is capable of taking care of us.

Of course, many people struggle with anxiety, and all of us are tempted to be afraid from time to time. God is merciful and gracious, comforting and soothing our fears as a mother comforts her small child. It's not wrong to have these feelings, but God wants to lead us through a process of healing and growth in which we learn to manage our fears by exercising our faith.

No one is a hero by birth. We are not courageous because we are supermen. Instead, our courage grows and flourishes through an awareness of God's love and trust in His unfailing promises. Each one of us can become more courageous by exercising faith in God.

If you wish to become more courageous, do not fix your eyes only on your problems. They can easily overwhelm you. Instead, look to

Him who is greater than any of your problems. Look to Him who is alive and powerful to save. Look to Him who is able to send you relief and to provide for you in more ways than you can even imagine. In the words of one of my favorite Christian authors, "Worry is blind, and cannot discern the future; but Jesus sees the end from the beginning. In every difficulty He has His way prepared to bring relief. Our heavenly Father has a thousand ways to provide for us, of which we know nothing. Those who accept the one principle of making the service and honor of God supreme will find perplexities vanish, and a plain path before their feet."[6]

Courage grows as we trust God's unfailing promises. Faith in His Word can make us strong, hopeful, and brave.

By the choices we make each day, each one of us can leave a legacy. My hope is that you will use your talents and skills not to impress other people, seeking earthly riches or recognition, but instead to practice faithfulness, kindness, and courage. Through these virtues, you can " 'love the LORD your God' . . . and 'your neighbor as yourself' " (Luke 10:27). This is a beautiful gift because "to love and be loved is to feel the sun from both sides."[7]

Reflection questions

1. In what areas do you find it difficult to be faithful to God? What are some specific ways that you would like to grow in your faithfulness?

2. Daniel is a good example of how one man's faithfulness influenced an entire kingdom. How might your faithfulness to God open doors for Him to show His faithfulness to those around you?

3. Mark Twain purportedly said, "Kindness is a language which the deaf can hear and the blind can see." What acts of kindness can you do this coming week?

4. In what areas of your life would you like to be more courageous? How can you move forward in faith?

1. David Viscott, *How to Live With Another Person* (New York: Arbor House, 1974), 25.

2. For a fascinating, faith affirming, and true story of my family and how they experienced God's protection and guidance during the challenging time of Nazi Germany, see Susi Hasel Mundy's book, *A Thousand Shall Fall: The Electrifying Story of a Soldier and His Family Who Dared to Practice Their Faith in Hitler's Germany* (Hagerstown, MD: Review and Herald®, 2001). If you have not read the book, I warn you: do not start reading it at night, just before you want to go to sleep, because the true stories are captivating and very faith uplifting. Once you start reading, it is difficult to put the book down.

3. Cf. the amazing story of Daniel in the Bible in the book of Daniel, chapter 6.

4. You can find more information about Bogenhofen at https://www.bogenhofen.at /en/sprachinstitut/.

5. Ellen G. White, *The Ministry of Healing* (Mountain View, CA: Pacific Press®, 1942), 470.

6. Ellen G. White, *The Desire of Ages* (Mountain View, CA: Pacific Press®, 1940), 330.

7. Viscott, *How to Live With Another Person,* 25.

Chapter 3

A Transforming Virtue: Waiting

Patience is a practice in trust.

—Unknown

In his classic children's book *Oh, the Places You'll Go,* Dr. Seuss warned his readers about getting stuck in a location that he called "The Waiting Place." According to Dr. Seuss, the people in the waiting place are perpetually

Waiting for a train to go
or a bus to come, or a plane to go
or the mail to come, or the rain to go
or the phone to ring, or the snow to snow
or waiting around for a Yes or No
or waiting for their hair to grow.
Everyone is just waiting.

Waiting for the fish to bite
or waiting for wind to fly a kite
or waiting around for Friday night
or waiting, perhaps, for their Uncle Jake
or a pot to boil, or a Better Break
or a string of pearls, or a pair of pants
or a wig with curls, or Another Chance.
Everyone is just waiting.[1]

We all know what it's like to wait. Whether young or old, male or female, rich or poor, married or single, every human being waits. We hope and dream—and we wait. We hunger and thirst—and wait. We experience suffering and pain—and wait for relief. We study and work—and wait for results. We pray—and wait for answers. We wait in line at the supermarket and gas station. We wait in traffic jams and at airports. We wait for the mail to arrive. We wait for good things to happen and bad things to go away. Some people wait at night to fall asleep, and some even wait to die.

We wait because God's grace has not ended

From birth to death, our lives are characterized by waiting. Sometimes the waiting is brief, and time passes quickly. Other times, the waiting lingers for many years.

Waiting can remind us that often, the most essential, most beautiful, and most lasting things in life are things beyond our control and power. And so we must learn to wait. Waiting is an essential practice of the virtuous life.

Waiting is intricately connected to the fact that God is alive. Because He lives, He relates to us in unexpected ways. Sometimes it is God's silence that seems the most startling. God's silence can be more challenging to us than what He says. Throughout Scripture, God is depicted as a Being who communicates, speaks, and reveals His will to human beings. This distinguishes Him as a personal God rather than an impersonal force or power. Yet there are times when God relates to us in silence.

As strange as it might sound, even God's silence is a sign of His personal nature. He is free to speak and also free to withhold His word. His silence is an expression of His personal sovereignty and freedom. We have to admit, however, that it's very difficult to wait for an answer from God only to experience silence.

I experienced this difficulty when my wife was diagnosed with terminal cancer in 2008. We waited in several hospitals before treatments began and after they ended. We waited for lab results to come in and for new appointments with the doctors. And where did we wait? In the waiting room, as the place is conveniently called.[2] We waited, both to see if treatment was working, and to discover how God would answer our prayers. I don't know about you, but I hate to wait. I don't like long lines, traffic jams, or delayed appointments. I get frustrated by tardy people and by processes that take longer than necessary. Waiting often seems like nothing more than a meaningless delay.

Unless you are an extremely patient person, you can probably relate to my aversion to waiting. But until we are in heaven, God calls us to wait. There is no human life without waiting. Because human beings exist in time, waiting is part of our identity, our story, and our history. There is no historical succession without waiting. Life as we know it would not exist without waiting. The person who lives—waits! The person who waits—lives! The paradox of the virtuous life is that waiting on God's timing is the most efficient way of living, even though it may feel like a waste of time.

Waiting upon God

Even the biblical writers knew about the experience of waiting. The prophets often expressed waiting with the question, "How long, O Lord?" (see Habakkuk 1:2; Daniel 8:13). The biblical authors also employed various word pictures that can only be understood in the context of waiting. For instance, the Bible speaks about hope. We have the wonderful Advent hope—that "looking for the blessed hope and glorious appearing of our great God and Savior Jesus Christ" (Titus 2:13). Hope and waiting are intimately connected. The person who hopes—waits! Then there is the patience of the saints: "Here is the patience of the saints; here are those who keep the commandments of God and the faith of Jesus" (Revelation 14:12). Perseverance and patience have to do with waiting. The person who is patient—waits!

Scripture also speaks about the longing of the believer for God, "As the deer pants for the water brooks, so pants my soul for You, O God" (Psalm 42:1). Longing is connected with waiting. The one who longs—waits!

Or consider Scripture's take on suffering. Suffering has to do with waiting. The suffering person often asks, "How long will it last, Lord Jesus?" The person who suffers—waits!

In the Bible, God also calls us to be alert and awake, so that we are ready when He returns (see 1 Peter 5:8; Luke 12:37). The person who is alert—waits!

In the final analysis, we all wait because God's grace has not yet ended! Even God, in His great mercy and patience, waits. He waits for us. He waits for you, and He waits for me. God does not want to lose anybody who could be saved. He waits to extend His grace and mercy to anyone who will accept it.

Waiting does not mean that we just sit passively—doing nothing, hoping that an unpleasant situation will somehow disappear. Neither does waiting mean blind optimism. To be optimistic and to have hope are not always the same thing. An optimist believes that circumstances will improve in the future: the weather, the economy, relationships, political challenges, and so on. By contrast, the hope which grows out of virtuous waiting trusts that God's promises will come true. Hope believes that God will keep His word because He is always faithful to what He has promised.

Thus, biblical hope is grounded in the trustworthy promises God has spoken in the past. Because God never changes, His word can be trusted. Therefore, we can have hope. God's faithfulness and truth guarantee this hope.

The path of hope goes back to the future, so to speak. The optimist focuses primarily on the future and believes everything will somehow get better. But the person who has hope remembers God's great faithfulness to His children in the past and His promises to remain faithful in the future. God's promises have been tried and tested many times throughout human history. This is the reason why we can live full of hope. Hope is not merely self-soothing. It is grounded and founded in God's loving faithfulness and truth.

The theater play *Waiting for Godot*, by Samuel Beckett, was named the "most significant English language play of the 20th century."[3] In it, two characters—the philosophical Vladimir and the weary Estragon—wait for the arrival of someone called named Godot. While waiting, they engage in a variety of meaningless discussions and encounter three other characters. But they do not know anything specific about this Godot and are not sure that he even exists at all. Godot never appears, and the wait for him is obviously in vain. The play runs in circles and ends in emptiness. It is utterly devoid of hope. In contrast to *Waiting for Godot*, biblical waiting is characterized by a living hope. Biblical hope does not end in emptiness and meaninglessness. Biblical hope has a specific goal. The living God of the prophetic word of Scripture is the center of our hope and gives meaning to our existence. Waiting for God is fundamentally different than *Waiting for Godot*.[4]

Waiting for answers

Who has not had this experience? You pray and wait for an answer. And you wait. And you pray. And you wait—for a very long time, and you don't seem to receive what you've been praying for. Even when we pray sincere prayers and, in our prayers, ask God for things He approves of, God still may let us wait. To persevere in prayer is a lesson that people through all ages have needed to learn.

God does not want us to be spiritual weaklings who are easily discouraged. This would cause us suffering and place us at risk for the enemy's attacks. Instead, God wants sincere, trusting people who confidently claim His promises and persevere in their prayers.

From a biblical perspective, the primary purpose of waiting is to bring to light who I am and who I am becoming while I wait. The experience of waiting confronts me with a significant spiritual decision: Do I allow my impatience and my doubts to question God's goodness and omnipotence? Or do I recognize that in waiting, I am confronted with a unique opportunity that will help me to become the person God desires me to be? Perhaps through waiting, I will become someone who I never would have been otherwise.

If we look at it this way, waiting becomes God's means of transforming us according to His will. Thus, waiting is truly an expression of God's goodness and grace. It helps us to become more like God, who waits in great patience, not wanting anyone to be lost who could still be saved.

While we are waiting for God to answer our prayers, worries and uncertainties may sneak up on us, especially when we have been praying for a long time, and the answer to our prayers is delayed.

During these times, it may be helpful to remember that we go through several stages while we wait for answers to our prayers.[5]

Intensity: The beginning of a prayer request is often characterized by a high degree of *intensity*. A crisis or special need may stimulate you to focus all your energy on asking God for help and for a clear solution to the problem. This is the first intensive stage.

Distraction: It is very difficult to maintain such an intense attitude of prayer over a longer period of time. Everyday life and essential daily transactions can inevitably distract your heart and thoughts. This will necessarily lead you to turn to other things that are essential for your living and survival. *Distraction* characterizes the second stage because, regardless of the importance of your prayer request, everyday life with its daily routine goes on.

Anger or impatience: In the third phase, you may experience *anger* or *impatience* because your desired answer does not appear in the form you had hoped for, or because it is delayed. When anger arises, it is often directed at God because it seems that He has not intervened or tried to help. Our anger may also turn toward the cause of the problem because the problem does not disappear and continues to cause distress. You may also feel angry with yourself because you are unable to do anything about the situation or might feel responsible for it.

Accusation: Anger often leads to a form of *accusation*. In this fourth phase of the waiting process, you may be tempted to reproach God: Why don't You act faster? Why is nothing happening? Why don't You step in to solve the problem? Accusations could also be turned toward others who you perceive to be the cause of the problem. Or you may accuse yourself because Satan, the accuser of all human beings, insinuates that God has delayed the answer to your prayer because you are so sinful or unworthy.

Discouragement: In the fifth phase, anger and accusation often lead to frustrations and *discouragement*. You may become uncertain whether or how you should continue to pray. If Satan succeeds in discouraging you, he has won the battle. God never discourages us. Instead, He longs to help us because He tenderly loves us! This important insight leads to the next phase.

Determination: If you don't let anger and frustration discourage you, you will advance to the next phase in which you *determine* to continue to pray. Sometimes you may feel like the man who calls out, "I believe; help my unbelief!" (Mark 9:24). Sometimes you might wrestle like Jacob and cry out, "I will not let You go unless You bless me!" (Genesis 32:26). Faith in this new phase is not so much a feeling but a conscious determination not to give up praying no matter how and when God will answer your prayer (Romans 12:12). This experience is possible only when you trust that God really is good and that He has kind intentions toward you. It pays to trust God and to wait on Him, "casting all your care upon Him, for He cares for you" (1 Peter 5:7). When your praying passes this test, the next phase is able to begin.

Joy and inner peace: Overcoming the temptation of discouragement in prayer opens the way for *rejoicing* in hope (Romans 12:12; 15:13; Philippians 4:4). A joyful faith, in turn, results in a heart that is filled with a *peace* that is higher than any human understanding. This is how you can learn to trust in God even if, from a human standpoint, you cannot imagine how God can accomplish the thing. The peace of God is grounded in the certainty that God's Word is dependable and deserves full acceptance (1 Timothy 1:15; 4:9; 2 Timothy 2:11; Hebrews 2:3).

In each of these stages, God's help is available to you! With His help, it is possible to have a new experience in your prayer life! Regardless of what your prayer life is like now, remember: It is *always* too soon to stop praying! It is *never* too late to start praying!

Waiting transforms

Waiting is difficult. But waiting without hope or meaning is almost unbearable. Only a person who has a worthy and meaningful goal in view can be patient and perseverant while waiting for it. The temptation in times of waiting is to focus on the things we wait for. We tend to focus on the obstacles that need to be removed or the good things that hopefully will bring change. But remember, waiting isn't just about what you are hoping for in the future. From a biblical perspective, waiting is also about who you can become as you wait, and how you can learn to trust God more fully. Waiting always presents you with a spiritual choice: Will you allow yourself to question God's goodness in what you experience, or will you embrace the opportunity of exercising living hope in times of waiting? Will you allow God to strengthen your trust in His goodness as you wait?

There are rich rewards for those who wait. My hope and prayer is that you will follow the example of the ancient King David, who wrote,

I would have lost heart, unless I had believed
That I would see the goodness of the LORD
In the land of the living.
Wait on the LORD;
Be of good courage,
And He shall strengthen your heart;
Wait, I say, on the LORD! (Psalm 27:13, 14).

Reflection questions

1. What are you waiting for at the moment? How may God be using this to transform you?
2. How does impatience with God, yourself, and others undermine the virtuous life?
3. How does it impact the way you live your life when you realize that God is waiting so that people may be saved?
4. Make a list of the blessings that come from waiting!
5. How many examples of waiting in the Bible can you think of? What lessons can you learn from these stories?

---

1. Dr. Seuss, *Oh, The Places You'll Go!* (New York: Random House, 1990), 23–25.

2. A waiting room is an architectural space whose sole purpose is to give room for people to wait. Often people are most receptive to encouraging thoughts or inspirational ideas while they have to wait during the time of uncertainty, waiting for the patient to receive the results of their test or to be admitted a new treatment. It is a pity how carelessly many waiting rooms are designed and how little is done to use this waiting time to make it a blessing.

3. Cf. "*Waiting for Godot,*" Wikipedia, accessed July 21, 2019, https://en.wikipedia.org /wiki/Waiting_for_Godot.

4. According to Beckett, the name should be pronounced with the emphasis on the first syllable: "GOD-oh," as it is done in France, England, and Ireland. Some see in the name a subtle reference to "God."

5. The stages are adapted from Ron Susek, "7 Waiting Phases," *Pray!*, no. 28, p. 18, as quoted in Dean Ridings, *The Pray! Prayer Journal* (Colorado Springs, CO: NavPress, 2003), 104, 105.

Chapter 4

The Enemy of Virtue: Envy

Envy is the art of counting the other
fellow's blessings instead of your own.

—Harold Coffin

I have an embarrassing story to share. Despite my passion for Christian virtue, and living the virtuous life, I'm still very human.

I remember vividly the excitement I felt when I started my work as a Bible teacher at Bogenhofen Seminary in Austria. The new work as a young teacher took all my energy. In addition to teaching theology, I had several other responsibilities on the side. Occasionally, I managed to find time to write an article for one of our church magazines. I thoroughly enjoyed my work and felt richly blessed. Well, at least I did at first.

But there was this *one other person* who started to interfere with my happiness: my cousin Michael Hasel. He started teaching the very same year I did, but instead of teaching at a small country school, Michael taught at a major university in the United States. He published articles in church magazines just as I did, but he also published several scientific articles in some of the most renowned and well-respected scholarly journals. This was something I could only dream about. Did I mention that Michael had also published a few books? I knew I could never keep up. It was even harder for me to accept that Michael was well connected and highly respected by some of the most prominent scholars in his field.

As I compared myself to Michael, I became frustrated and

discouraged. As a young, aspiring scholar, I knew that publications were extremely important for the academic reputation I wanted to build. Publications could significantly impact my professional future and career. This was important to me!

Instead of celebrating my cousin's accomplishments, I started to hold a grudge. Eventually, the grudge started to hold me. I secretly envied Michael's success. I coveted the superior academic work environment he was in, the better research library, the sabbaticals he had, the professional allowances, and all the other advantages that were helping him "get ahead." I envied him for the things I didn't have. The more I started to compare myself with Michael, the more our relationship suffered. It certainly was not *his* fault. It was *my* problem.

Have you ever been caught in the trap of envy? It is easy to wish that we could be just as talented, successful, wealthy, popular, attractive, articulate, or well respected as the people we see around us. Do you compare yourself often with others? Are you unhappy with yourself? Do you often have the feeling that you are disadvantaged, overlooked, or missing out on something you actually deserve?

There are a variety of sins whose damaging effects weigh heavily on us, undermining the virtuous life. Envy is a sin that almost all of us struggle with to a certain degree. Many characters in the Bible shared this struggle. From the beginning, Cain and Abel were confronted with it. Joseph and his brothers had to deal with it. Both the Old and New Testaments warn against envy. We could say that envy is obsession *par excellence*.

This universal problem can cause serious damage to our characters and our relationships. Spiritually minded people are not immune to envy. Therefore, it's important to understand and guard against this sin if we want to experience the pleasure of virtue.

Envy

Because He knew the danger of envy, God dedicated an entire

commandment to this sin. His warning against covetousness is the final chord in the melody of the Decalogue. This commandment doesn't just deal with our deeds but reaches into our very thoughts!

Envy is a malicious and nagging inner disposition to jealously covet the success, advantages, or possessions of another person. Envy is often accompanied by very powerful feelings. These feelings can be so destructive that an envious person is inclined to devalue the other person in their mind. In its mildest form, envy can cause discontent and frustration. In extreme cases, envy may lead to theft or other crimes.

Envy is a form of blindness in which I can no longer realistically see my own gifts, or the blessings God has given me. Instead, my perception is intensely focused on the achievements, possessions, or strengths of others.

The view of envy,
to the dismay of all,
sees all the other things as big and strong,
but all my own achievements small.[1]

Thus, envy narrows our field of vision. Consequently, we build walls that separate us from one another, and ultimately even from God. We become prisoners of our own feelings of deprivation.

Envy is one of the most mysterious sins. It led to the origin of all evil in the universe when Lucifer envied a position he did not have. The root of our envy is as tragic as it is human: it grows in the soil of our own deficit. It grows out of a feeling of deprivation in which we believe one of the following things:

- I must attain or accomplish something else in order to be acceptable and valuable.
- I have not received what I deserve, while others have received more than they deserve.

- I have been treated unfairly compared to others, and this must be corrected.

Envy makes our hearts bitter. This bitterness leads to strife, controversy, and "every evil thing," as we read in James 3:16, "For where envy and self-seeking exist, confusion and every evil thing are there." The modern Bible translation *The Message* describes it this way, "Whenever you're trying to look better than others or get the better of others, things fall apart and everyone ends up at the others' throats."

Envy leads to chaos and confusion. However, the apostle Paul has told us that "God is not the author of confusion but of peace" (1 Corinthians 14:33). This idea is echoed in James 3:17: "But the wisdom that is from above is first pure, then peaceable, gentle, willing to yield, full of mercy and good fruits, without partiality and without hypocrisy."

Envy is never satisfied. It never gets enough! Envy is strong and powerful but makes us weak. Have you heard the expression "green with envy"? Envy can even have physiological symptoms. Until the early 1900s, envy was dreaded like the plague and actually considered a disease. Physicians in the early 1900s believed that envy could be recognized by the yellowish color of a patient's eyes, the paleness of the face, and even the discoloration of the derrière, or buttocks. These premodern diagnostic criteria were eventually dismissed as obsolete, but envy hasn't become obsolete. It grows all around us, like a powerful weed, choking out the flowers in the garden of life.

As the wise King Solomon aptly stated, "Envy is rottenness to the bones" (Proverbs 14:30). Envy makes us sick. It isolates us from our fellow human beings.

God knows all about the destructive power of envy. He understands what we are jealous of and why. That's why He included the final commandment to protect us. The words of the tenth commandment read as follows: "You shall not covet your neighbor's wife; and you shall not desire your neighbor's house, his field, his male servant, his female servant, his ox, his donkey, or anything that is your neighbor's" (Deuteronomy 5:21).

There are seven specific things we are told not to covet. The number seven seems to indicate completeness. By listing these seven items, God seemed to be representing all the various types of property a person could own (or could covet). Why then, after this inclusive list, did He add the final clause: "or anything that is your neighbor's"?

A brief Hebrew lesson will help us understand. The word translated into English as "anything" is the short Hebrew word *kól*. *Kól* can mean "anything" as we understand the word, but in the Hebrew language, it can also denote the entirety or totality of something.

It seems that God was trying to tell us, "You shall not covet your neighbor's wife; and you shall not covet your neighbor's house, his field, his male servant, his female servant, his ox, his donkey, or everything else, that is, the totality of all that is your neighbor's!"

Here we discover something fascinating about the way God views us as human beings. God always sees us comprehensively. We often covet this or that in the life of another person. It's easy to envy individual things. But God sees the liabilities that come along with each blessing. The question He wants us to ask ourselves is "Do I really want *everything* this other person has?"

Not just the attractive and beautiful wife of your neighbor, but also the mother-in-law and extended family that go along with her!

Not just the big house of your neighbor, but also the large mortgage payments, utility bills, and property taxes that go along with it!

Not just the money the other person has, but also the burden of the responsibility for the money!

Not just the impressive German sports car of your neighbor, but also the exorbitant leasing and insurance payments to drive it!

Not just the success in one's professional career, but also the hard and enduring work that made it possible!

Not just the sweet cherries from your neighbor's garden, but also the time-consuming care for the garden and its produce!

In other words, do you really want *everything*—that is, the totality of it all? Do you want to trade the life God has given you with your neighbor's *entire life*? Would you be willing to live in his or her skin *completely*? It is this totality of life that God has in view. He loves us as individuals and wants to safeguard the unique lives and blessings that He has given each one of us.

Life is not a shopping spree. The tenth commandment makes it clear that life does not work that way. We often notice and envy only the attractive things in other people's lives: the success, the talents, the money, the beautiful houses, the fast cars, and the admiration they receive from others. But God sees everything! He knows our unique histories and is familiar with every single aspect of our lives. He knows us from birth. He knows all the successes and failures, the challenges and blessings, the joys and sorrows we have experienced.

Just as trees have rings that chronicle their histories, our lives unfold like rings on a tree. Every year gives each one of us a unique identity and history that no one else has. This individual history cannot be compartmentalized or dissected.

We can benefit from seeing each other in this totality. If I pick only a few precious things from the life of my neighbor, if I isolate and covet only what is desirable in my eyes, I will not see my neighbor's life or my own accurately. In my mind, I will cut something from the life of the other person that may have taken years to grow. I will also try to imagine something into my own life that may not be congruent with God's specific will for me. We often fail to realize that the things we envy would not fit smoothly into our own lives or histories. By guarding us against envy, God is actually giving us freedom to be ourselves, while allowing others to be themselves too.

Only as I start to see other people in their entirety—as people who, through their whole lives and through God's grace, have become what they are—will I then see them as God sees them.

We must remember that every human being experiences a variety of blessings and disappointments, gains and losses, successes and failures. In order to be content, we must learn to let go of things we would love to have but don't. We can see our disappointments as opportunities to turn our minds and hearts toward heavenly realities, remembering that this world is not our home.

We cannot have everything in life. We must deal with this painful reality by letting go, mourning, and then accepting it. Envy hinders this important work of grieving. The person who is jealous is at a tremendous disadvantage—blind to the blessings they have, and unable to celebrate the blessings or contributions of others.

Envy makes us incapable of enjoying what we have. However, with God's help, we can learn to focus on the customized, personalized blessings God has given us. We can also find new ways to put our own unique abilities and resources to good use.

It's easy to waste time being discontent and comparing ourselves with others. But comparison leads to two equally harmful results: either we become depressed, or we become proud. Both are a hindrance to the work of the Holy Spirit in our lives and hearts! Often it is not our poverty or the deficiencies we experience that hinder the influence of God's grace in our lives, but instead our resistance to accept the lives God has given us and to use the resources we already have to His glory.

The rest of my story

When I finally realized God's personalized blessings in my own life, I started to breathe again, spiritually speaking. I told God about the things I missed. I told him about my unfulfilled dreams, my disappointments, my deficiencies, and my inner longings. As I did this, I experienced the miraculous wonder of God's transforming grace. Slowly, I was able to accept (with God's help) the actual life in which I found myself.

God opened my eyes to the many blessings I had and the things I could use for His glory. This perspective provided a window for me to view my cousin Michael differently. I was able to be grateful for his blessings and even rejoice with him in his success. I realized that I experienced greater joy and satisfaction in my own life when I let go of envy. With God's help, I started to see Michael in his totality and to view his success and knowledge as something that could enrich our relationship. I also realized that God had created me to contribute to His work and to His people in ways that were uniquely suited for me. The same is true for each one of us.

When God looks at you, He doesn't focus on a single strength or a single deficiency. He sees all of you. He sees you from beginning to end, and values you like no other person in the universe. God doesn't want you to be someone else. By accepting His custom blessings for you, instead of comparing yourself with others, you will become more and more like Jesus—and more and more like the person He created you to be.

Reflection questions:

1. Think of a time when you were envious or jealous. How did you feel and how did you deal with those feelings? What do you wish you had done differently?
2. In what ways does envy blind you to your God-given value and abilities?
3. How can envy limit your horizons and potential?
4. What is the best antidote to envy?
5. Pause and ask God to help you with any feelings of envy you may have at this moment.

---

1. This is my English translation of a German poem by Friedrich Rückert, "Der Blick des Neides sieht zu seiner eignen Pein nur alles Fremde groß und alles Eigene klein" *Die Weisheit des Brahmanen, ein Lehrgedicht in Bruchstücken*, vol. 5 (Leipzig: 1839), 89.

Chapter 5

The Underrated Virtue: Humility

'Tis a gift to be simple
'Tis a gift to be free
'Tis a gift to come down where we ought to be.
—Shaker hymn

Humility is the first of the virtues—for other people.
—Oliver Wendell Holmes Sr.

Have you ever wondered where the expression "eating humble pie" came from? What does humility have to do with pie? Interestingly enough, this phrase was not originally about a metaphorical pie but a literal one! In the middle ages, "umble" pie was a dish made out of the innards of a deer or other animals—the liver, heart, intestines, and other organs. Umble pie was eaten by the common people, but not the wealthy. Eventually, it started being referred to as "humble pie," and the expression was born.

Whether literal or metaphorical, humble pie is difficult to swallow. No one is naturally humble. Of all the virtues of the human heart, humility is one of the most elusive, and perhaps the most difficult to attain. Pride comes to us as naturally as breathing.

Our western culture is nearly devoid of humility. Rather than encouraging meekness, it rewards arrogance and conceit. People thriving on acts of self-promotion and greatness seem anything but humble. As the famous world-class boxer and world heavyweight champion Muhammad Ali is reported to have said, "It is hard to be humble when you're as great as I am."[1] But even for those who are not "the greatest," humility is a rare commodity. To make it worse, few people even realize they're missing it.

Humility is often misunderstood. Some view it as a weak and passive attribute, characterized by a lack of energy, ambition, and confidence. For many people, humility seems to threaten the possibility of impressive achievement. Successful people are tempted to avoid humility because they don't understand the true power and beauty of it. In reality, humility is an amazing strength. In a very real sense, it is the crown of all virtues and the foundation of all true knowledge.[2]

The value of humility

The story is told of Demosthenes, the great Greek orator. One day he was asked by one of his students to identify the most important aspect of public speaking. He replied that it was the delivery or articulation. This makes sense, because the best sermons, most brilliant thoughts, and most powerful arguments will all be useless unless delivered and articulated clearly.

Demosthenes was then asked to describe the second most important aspect of public speaking. His answer was again articulation. And the third most important aspect? Articulation. After sharing this story, the ancient church father Augustine raised the crucial question: "What is the most important aspect of the Christian religion?" Augustine responded: it is humility. And what is the second most important aspect? Humility! And what is the third most important aspect? Humility! Augustine believed that humility was the only way to live a virtuous life.

"This way is first humility, second humility, third humility, and however often you should ask me I would say the same, not because there are not other precepts to be explained, but, *if humility does not precede* and *accompany* and *follow* every good work we do, and *if it is not set before us to look upon,* and *beside us to lean upon,* and *behind us to fence us in,* pride will wrest from our hand any good deed we do while we are in the very act of taking pleasure in it."[3]

Humility and value

Without humility, pride will sneak in and spoil every good act of which we are capable. As rare as true humility is today, God has never stopped valuing it. Therefore, He is committed to helping us grow in humility. He demonstrated what it means to be humble when He humbled Himself for all to see in the person of Jesus Christ (Philippians 2:5–11). Humility does not mean that we should think poorly of ourselves. Instead, true humility grows out of an understanding of God's love for us as His children. It provides a loving awareness of who we are, who others are, and who God is. Humility sets us free from the exhausting struggle to define our worth based on our accomplishments. "Humility means we do not think more highly of ourselves than we ought because we know ourselves in light of God (see Romans 12:3)."[4] Understood that way, humility opens the door to grow in grace. Grace is not the liberty to do as we please but is the power to live as we ought. Grace is God's gift to live a Christlike life. God told us that He gives grace to the humble, and He actively opposes the proud person (Proverbs 3:34; James 4:6; 1 Peter 5:5).

God has gifted each one of us with valuable skills and talents. He wants us to strive for excellence. Humility doesn't contradict this fact but simply reminds us that our Creator is the One who gives us the ability to succeed, for the purpose of blessing others, glorifying Him, and experiencing joy.

To live humbly is a virtue. It is also an act of the will. Each one of us must choose between the lasting pleasure of humility and the inevitable pain of pride.

The problem with pride

Nothing good results from pride. It alienates us from our fellow human beings and makes us self-sufficient. It's impossible to believe we are better than others without simultaneously experiencing disconnection from them. Pride can creep into our lives through our possessions, our success, our knowledge, our thinking, or a multitude of other means. But regardless of its form, pride is always damaging.

Pride can be recognized in our conversations. As we speak with others, pride may tempt us to monopolize the conversation. Sometimes we spend too much time sharing our own opinions and dwelling on our own experiences rather than exploring the needs or thoughts of others. Humility in conversation will lead us to show interest and care in the people with whom we converse.

Proud people, on the other hand, often are argumentative and create discord and strife through their interaction. Ultimately, pride leads not to humility but rather to the humiliation of the other person.[5] It leads us to take all the credit for our successes, neglecting to acknowledge the important contributions of others. It has a corrupting influence.

Because it is essentially competitive in nature, pride prevents us from enjoying the insights and achievements of others. Instead, it builds walls of suspicion and resentment between us and the very people whose thoughts and gifts could enrich us.[6] Humility protects our relationships by reminding us that our talents were given to us by God, and also by encouraging us to notice the gifts and talents He has given to others. In this way, humility can make life less like a competition and more like a symphony.

The proud person does not feel the need to learn from others. The proud person already knows. This is why proud people find making friends so difficult and why they are difficult to get along with, but humble people make very pleasant company. Humility offers the promise of excellence in many ways. "Humble persons do not threaten or challenge another's rights, nor do they claim more for themselves than has been duly allotted them in life."[7] A humble person does not attempt to better themself at the expense of others, to acquire more than others do, or to strive for honor that others currently enjoy.

Proud people, in contrast, enjoy being served rather than serving others. They are unable to receive feedback without becoming defensive. Proud people would rather humiliate others than humble themselves. This makes pride a serious handicap to any leadership, because it minimizes, degrades, and undermines those who are being led.[8]

Pride can even bring down nations. One example of this is the ancient Roman Empire, which, as the superpower of the world at that time, was thought to be indomitable. No one imagined that Rome would be conquered by barbarian tribes. Nonetheless, the empire's prosperity and pride led to corruption, diminishing its power and making it vulnerable to defeat. According to historian and author Edward Gibbon, Rome eventually experienced its demise because "immoderate greatness caused it to fall."[9] The story of Rome validates Scripture's claim, "Pride goes before destruction, and a haughty spirit before a fall" (Proverbs 16:18).

Humility and wisdom

Pride stifles the imagination and prevents people from listening, learning, and growing. It prevents people from becoming what they could be. By contrast, humble people accept that they don't know everything. They do not see themselves as owners of truth but rather stewards of it. Humble people are free to be curious rather than cynical. This prepares them to be lifelong learners, gaining valuable insights from the people around them.

Humility also makes us more receptive to truth. It reminds us that we are dependent on wisdom and help outside of ourselves. Christians who cultivate humility by learning and following the truths of God's Word will expand their understanding of the world and of reality in ways that proud people never can. It has been aptly stated, "Humility enables courage and points wisdom in the right direction. It is the backbone of temperance, and it makes love possible."[10]

Humility in Scripture

The Bible has much to say about humility. It urges us to do nothing out of selfish ambition, but to place the interests of others ahead of our own (Philippians 2:3, 4). It encourages us to have the humble mind of Christ (verse 5; cf. Romans 12:2; 1 Corinthians 2:16), who followed the path of humility in order to save us. It teaches that humility leads to a recognition of one's own sinfulness (Isaiah 6:5).

The Bible teaches that humility will lead to voluntary submission to God (2 Chronicles 34:27) as well as to those God has placed in positions of authority in our lives. Scripture reveals six types of authority-submission relationships. According to Christian leadership expert Tom Yeakley, these include: "God and mankind, government and citizens, employer and employee, husband and wife, parents and children, and spiritual leaders and followers. How we submit to these divinely placed authorities in our lives reveals either humility or pride."[11] Of course, it's important to remember that we should never obey an authority figure who is asking us to do something that contradicts God's Word. We also must create appropriate boundaries when authority figures are abusive or unsafe.

Following the example of Jesus

The prophet Micah wrote one of the most concise descriptions of God's desire for His people:

> He has shown you, O man, what is good;
> And what does the LORD require of you
> But to do justly,
> to love mercy,
> And *to walk humbly* with your God? (Micah 6:8; emphasis added).

No one has ever done as justly, loved as mercifully, or walked as humbly as Jesus Christ. Because of His great love for us, Jesus "humbled Himself and became obedient to the point of death, even the death of the cross" (cf. Philippians 2:5–11). Jesus was exalted and glorified through humility and love. His example teaches us that the only way up is down.

Humility goes against the current of our culture and the deep-seated pride in every human heart. But as you cultivate this virtue, your life will become much richer and more rewarding than it ever could be otherwise. Your relationships will improve, your mind will expand, and your capacity to enjoy God's blessings will exponentially increase.

Reflection questions

1. Reflect on the six authority-submission relationships mentioned on page 58. Which do you find the most difficult, and why?
2. Are there areas in your life and relationships in which pride is building barriers? How can you break down those barriers?
3. What is the source of true humility?
4. How can you be a better steward of truth?
5. What are the benefits of a humble lifestyle?

---

1. Muhammad Ali in Arlene Schulman and Martha Cosgrove, *Muhammad Ali* (Minneapolis, MN: Lerner Publishing Group, 2005), 47, as quoted in David J. Bobb, *Humility: An Unlikely Biography of America's Greatest Virtue* (Nashville, TN: Thomas Nelson, 2013), 5.

2. Cf. chapter 1.

3. Augustine of Hippo, Letter 115, in *Letters (83–130)*, ed. Roy Joseph Deferrari, trans. Wilfrid Parsons, vol. 18, *The Fathers of the Church* (Washington, DC: The Catholic University of America Press, 1953), 282; emphasis added.

4. Tom Yeakley, *Growing Kingdom Character: Practical, Intentional Tools for Developing Leaders* (Colorado Springs, CO: NavPress, 2011), 56.

5. Kevin Vanhoozer, *Is There a Meaning in This Text? The Bible, the Reader, and the Morality*

of Literary Knowledge (Grand Rapids, MI: Zondervan, 1998), 463.

6. Philip E. Dow, *Virtuous Minds: Intellectual Character Development* (Downers Grove, IL: InterVarsity Press, 2013), 74.

7. Bruce J. Malina and Mark Allan Powell, "Humility," in Mark Allan Powell, ed., *The HarperCollins Bible Dictionary (Revised and Updated)* (New York: HarperCollins, 2011), 397.

8. Yeakley, *Growing Kingdom Character*, 64.

9. Edward Gibbon, *The History of the Decline and Fall of the Roman Empire*, vol. 2, ed. David Womersley (New York: Penguin, 1994), 509.

10. David Bobb, *Humility: An Unlikely Biography of America's Greatest Virtue* (Nashville, TN: Thomas Nelson, 2013), 6.

11. Yeakley, *Growing Kingdom Character*, 59.

Chapter 6

The Virtue of Gratitude

Gratitude . . . turns what we have into enough.
—Melody Beattie

After my wife died, I kind of stopped noticing colors for some time. We had always enjoyed the fall colors together. Autumn was her favorite season of the year, but without her by my side, the leaves just didn't seem colorful anymore. Instead, everything looked gray and bland. The places we had once enjoyed together seemed unattractive without her. The songs I had once sung sounded meaningless. The future I had once envisioned seemed empty. Like many people grieving the death of a loved one, I was so focused on what I had lost that it was difficult for me to notice or appreciate the blessings I still had. To be completely honest, the last thing I wanted to practice was gratitude.

King Solomon wrote,

> To everything there is a season,
> A time for every purpose under heaven: . . .
>
> A time to weep,
> And a time to laugh;
> A time to mourn,
> And a time to dance (Ecclesiastes 3:1, 4).

God understands that we cycle through different emotions. We can come to Him in sorrow, joy, anger, or fear—and be completely honest with Him about how we are feeling. He will respond with compassion and kindness. But regardless of the circumstances and conflicting emotions of our lives, God still wants us to practice gratitude. He knows that gratitude will remind us of His love and power and will enhance the quality of our lives.

My aunt Hilde modeled gratitude to me in a beautiful way. She could relate to my pain because her husband had died in a tragic car accident some years earlier. But she chose to remain grateful and challenged me to do the same. She encouraged me to do a simple gratitude exercise that I found very helpful. Each day for a week, I was to write down ten words of things I was grateful for as well as ten sentences explaining why I was grateful for each thing. These sentences could even be turned into prayers. For example:

- *Eyes.* Thank You, Lord, for my eyes, because they allow me to see color and the faces of people I love.
- *Hands.* Thank You, God, for my hands, which allow me to write, to do good, and to touch other people.
- *Toothbrush.* Thank You, Lord, for my toothbrush, because it helps my mouth to feel fresh and clean, which also helps give me confidence.

When I first started the practice, it was challenging to know what to write. But gratitude is like a muscle; the more you exercise it, the stronger it grows. At the end of the week, I had seventy things to be grateful for, but I also had a new perspective. Instead of focusing on what I didn't have, I had increased my capacity to enjoy the "hidden" blessings that had been there all along.

Do you have any "hidden blessings" that you could enjoy more? Do you feel burdened and frustrated with the negative or unfair aspects of life? If so, perhaps gratitude can bless you like it has blessed me.

God has invited and called His children to be people who exercise gratitude. "In everything give thanks; for this is God's will for you in Christ Jesus," the apostle Paul writes in 1 Thessalonians 5:18 (NASB). Giving thanks means remembering that someone has done something good for us and expressing that goodness in words. God wants us to express our gratitude for the life He has given us and the many beautiful things He has created for us to enjoy.[1]

On this side of eternity, life will never run smoothly or perfectly. But it doesn't have to be perfect to be beautiful! Beauty meets and greets us unlike anything else in the world. It startles us in breathtaking ways, moving our minds and hearts to consider its Source. The fragrant smell of a rose, the majestic waves crashing on the shore, the affectionate twinkle in a friend's eyes—each experience of beauty echoes God's love and reminds us of the beautiful things He has prepared for those who love Him.

Like goodness, beauty is part of God's created reality. Although it surrounds us, it's something we often miss.[2] Developing an attitude of gratitude will open our eyes to the beautiful things in nature, the lovely people, and the wonderful experiences in life that we often overlook. Gratitude allows us to be thankful for the simple blessings and valuable people around us, without demanding perfection or satisfaction all the time.[3] Interestingly, the word *gratitude* is derived from the Latin word *gratia,* which means grace, graciousness, or gratefulness.

By practicing gratitude, virtuous people shift their attention from the imaginary things they don't have to the reality of the blessings they do (still) have. Gratitude grows out of an awareness of God's generosity and a curiosity to explore the specific ways He has shown His love to us. Such gratitude widens the horizon of life and increases our capacity to experience pleasure.

Instead of focusing on the things we lack or the things we are unable to do, we can deliberately reflect on the many things we *do have* and *are able* to do. Gratitude fosters a mind-set that brings

satisfaction in its wake. It also raises our awareness of the many opportunities and possibilities we have to share God's blessings with others.
This can be as simple as sharing a smile, expressing appreciation, or
doing a random act of kindness.

A *Harvard Health Publications* article has aptly stated that gratitude
is the healthiest emotion of all. "In positive psychology research, gratitude is strongly and consistently associated with greater happiness.
Gratitude helps people feel more positive emotions, relish good experiences, improve their health, deal with adversity, and build strong
relationships. Most studies published on this topic have found an
association between gratitude and an individual's well-being."[4] Other
research has confirmed these remarkable findings.

Dr. Martin E. P. Seligman, a leading researcher and psychologist at
the University of Pennsylvania, scientifically tested the impact of various gratitude exercises on over four hundred people. While gratitude
journaling proved to be beneficial, another practice was even more
powerful. Participants received an assignment to write and personally deliver a letter of gratitude to a person who had contributed
to their lives but had never been properly thanked for his or her
kindness. After delivering their letters, participants immediately
exhibited a huge increase in happiness scores. The study showed that
the impact was greater than that of any other gratitude intervention.
These positive effects lasted for a month.[5] No wonder God calls us to
express our thankfulness—He knows it will bring us joy and will be
a blessing to those around us.

Imagine the tremendous benefits you can receive as you cultivate
an attitude of gratitude: positive emotions, memories of good experiences, increased physical and mental health, stronger relationships,
and increased resilience to cope with adverse situations. These benefits
are well worth the minimal effort required to practice gratitude.

Giving thanks indeed changes life for the better. I can personally
testify to this. Learning to be thankful and to express gratitude

following the death of my wife, Ulrike, was probably one of the most difficult things I have ever learned, but it opened up a perspective that has transformed my life for the better. He who gives thanks lives not only more gratefully, but also more contentedly and healthfully. Gratitude leads to peace and contentment. According to a wise Amish proverb, "Contentment is not getting what we want but being satisfied with what we have."[6]

My aunt challenged me to practice gratitude, and I want to challenge you. Every day for the next week, write down ten things for which you are grateful. You can start your list on the next page. After you have written down ten words (e.g., eyes, bed, friend, etc.), think for a moment about what these things actually mean to you (e.g., What do my eyes mean for me? What do they enable me to do that I wouldn't be able to do if I were blind? What does my bed mean to me? How would life change if I always had to sleep on a hard, cold floor? What does my friend mean to me? How would life be different if I didn't have this friend in my life?).

Then, take each word and write a short sentence expressing your gratitude to God, the Giver of "every good gift and every perfect gift" (James 1:17). You can say, "Lord Jesus, thank You for my eyes with which I can see colors and read books. Thank You for my bed that keeps me comfortable and warm. Thank You for my supportive friend that makes life so much more enjoyable. Thank You for . . ."

Next, speak each of these sentences out loud so that you can hear your own voice. The more you engage your senses (seeing, touching, speaking, hearing) in expressing thankfulness, the more firmly the grateful thoughts will be fixed in your mind.

The next day, repeat the process with ten new things. If you want to intensify this exercise, repeat the items from the previous day (or days). At the end of just one week, you will already have seventy reasons to be grateful! If you keep building the habit, gratitude will change your life—guaranteed!

Reflection challenge

1. Try the gratitude exercise for a week. See what happens.
2. Engage as many senses as possible: write it; see it; read it; speak it; hear it. If it's food, you can even taste it!
3. Write and deliver a letter of gratitude to someone who has made a difference in your life.

---

1. If you want to listen to a stimulating talk on gratitude and the beauty of nature, Louie Schwartzberg, "Nature. Beauty. Gratitude," TED, accessed November 7, 2019, https://www .ted.com/talks/louie_schwartzberg_nature_beauty_gratitude?language=en.

2. On the startling presence of beauty in this world, read the stimulating thoughts in Gregory E. Ganssle, *Our Deepest Desire: How the Christian Story Fulfills Human Aspirations* (Downers Grove, IL: InterVarsity Press, 2017), 73–76.

3. Cf. Suzanne Wood Fischer, *The Heart of the Amish: Life Lessons on Peacemaking and the Power of Forgiveness* (Grand Rapids, MI: Revell, 2012), 162.

4. Harvard Medical School, "In Praise of Gratitude," *Harvard Health Publications,* November 2011, http://www.health.harvard.edu/newsletters/Harvard_Mental_Health_Letter/2011 /November/in-praise-of-gratitude, as quoted in Fischer, *The Heart of the Amish,* 162, 176.

5. M. E. P. Seligman et al., "Empirical Validation of Interventions," *American Psychologist* 60, no. 1 (July–August 2005): 410–421, as quoted in Fischer, *The Heart of the Amish,* 163, 176.

6. Fischer, *The Heart of the Amish,* 160.

Chapter 7

The Virtue of Prayer

Prayer is not conquering God's reluctance,
but taking hold upon God's willingness.

—Phillips Brooks

We all know that prayer is important. The Bible tells story after story of the power of prayer to accomplish the impossible. We've been taught that prayer can calm our fears, give us peace, and provide strength to resist temptation. We've learned that prayer can literally change people, dramatically alter the course of events, and even subdue demonic forces. We know that our prayers can help us to be more effective in our work for God and can bless the lives of the people we love.

Prayer is as essential for our spiritual life as breathing is for our physical life. Prolific Christian author Ellen White describes it this way: "Prayer is the opening of the heart to God as to a friend. Not that it is necessary in order to make known to God what we are, but in order to enable us to receive Him. Prayer does not bring God down to us, but brings us up to Him."[1]

We know so much about prayer! Yet often, we do not pray. We know that prayer is essential to Christian virtue, yet we frequently ignore the practice. The paradox of prayer is that while we desperately need it, we often eagerly avoid it.

Perhaps we've become bored by following dull routines of asking God again and again to help us and fulfill our wishes. Perhaps we use repetitious prayer phrases out of habit. The shallow and superficial words we say have lost their transforming power and diminished our grip on God. We know intellectually that we can ask God for many blessings—nothing is impossible for Him. However, in reality, our prayer lives look very different.

I distinctly remember a young student who heard me present "The ABC's of Biblical Prayer"[2] to a group of young people in her church. About three weeks later, she approached me, looking quite upset. "It doesn't work," she said. "What you told us is not true!"

When I asked her what had happened, she told me her story. This young lady shared an apartment with another young woman who had a distinctly different sense of cleanliness and order. Her roommate left piles of dirty dishes for days at a time, rarely picked up after herself, and seemed perfectly content to spread her mess throughout the apartment.

When this young woman heard my prayer talk, she thought she had found the answer. Rather than working to improve her relationship with her roommate or to address the issue kindly and directly, she simply started praying that her roommate would become more orderly. If the prayers "worked," she would not have to change herself to become more patient or more effective in her communication. Instead, her roommate would change to accommodate her level of cleanliness and comfort.

It is not wrong to pray for other people. God calls us to pray for the conversion and well-being of others, even our enemies. It's not wrong to pray that the people around us will be inspired to adopt better habits.

But could it be that the majority of our prayers are motivated by our own convenience rather than love for God or love for others? Could it be that we are missing out on opportunities to experience God's presence and His blessings because our prayers focus more on our problems than on Him?

All too often, we place ourselves at the center of our prayers, rather than placing God at the center. All too often, we use prayer as a spiritual vending machine, where our "want to have" list dominates the conversation.

The Bible contains a promise that I believe should inform the way we pray. It says, "Delight yourself in the LORD; and He will give you the desires of your heart" (Psalm 37:4, NASB). As our Creator, God knows what we want and need much better than we do. We assume we know what the desires of our hearts are, so we bring those desires to God and ask Him to give them to us. But according to this text, the prerequisite to receiving the real desires of our hearts is to delight ourselves in God. This should be the first goal of prayer.

When the disciples asked Jesus to teach them how to pray, He began The Lord's Prayer with a sentence of delight in God: "Our Father which art in heaven, hallowed be thy name" (Matthew 6:9, KJV). Before the disciples presented any requests or asked for forgiveness, they were instructed to marvel in and express the goodness of God's character. Jesus knew that this practice would put them in the right frame of mind to pray properly. Instead of focusing our prayers primarily on our own requests, I believe we need to refocus on God and make Him central in our thoughts and words. To seek and enjoy God's presence in prayer is much more valuable than simply seeking His blessings.

The story is told of the father of Adolf Schlatter, a renowned New Testament scholar who taught in Germany. When Schlatter's father was lying on his deathbed, one of his friends tried to console him by asking whether he was looking forward to the New Jerusalem's pearly gates, dazzling streets of gold, and spectacular crystal sea. The dying man looked at him incredulously and gave a remarkable answer: "Away with such rubbish!" he said. "All I want is to be in the Father's bosom."[3]

As human beings, we are created in the image of Christ, who

wants us to relate to God in the close and intimate way that He does. Describing this close connection, the apostle John wrote, "No one has seen God at any time. *The only begotten Son, who is in the bosom of the Father,* He has declared Him" (John 1:18; emphasis added). Shortly before His death, Jesus prayed that His disciples and all of His followers in the future (including you) would have a similar close connection with God: " 'I have declared to them Your name, and will declare it, that the love with which You loved Me may be in them, and I in them' " (John 17:26).

We were not created to relate to God as a vending machine, but rather as an affectionate Father who ministers to us as we come close to His side. We are invited to rest in His bosom. This connection should be the primary goal of our prayers.[4] Such prayer begins with personal communion with God and admiration of who He is, rather than simply a list of wishes and requests. When our wishes are not anchored in a living relationship with God, they may not be in harmony with His will. We can easily become confused about our desires, forgetting that God knows what we want and need better than we do.

As we allow communion with God and adoration of His character to become the central hub of our prayers, prayer will take on a much richer meaning. We will begin to think and pray from God's perspective. It will be easier to view our requests, wishes, and challenges through His eyes.

Several Bible characters modeled this type of prayer for us, giving us powerful examples to emulate. When a great multitude of enemies threatened to destroy Judah, King Jehoshaphat knew he was powerless to prevail against the forces of evil. All he could do was pray. But he didn't start his prayer by expressing his great need for help or asking God to intervene. Instead, he first focused on God's goodness and power. He recounted God's faithfulness by retelling His saving acts to the children of Israel in past history. (If you have even four minutes, I encourage you to read the prayer for yourself in 2 Chronicles 20:5–12.) After confidently reminding God (and himself) of God's faithfulness, Jehoshaphat expressed the urgent need. He ended the prayer with the dependence and confidence of a child, "For we have no power against this great multitude that is coming against us; nor do we know what to do, but our eyes are upon You" (2 Chronicles 20:12).

Rather than focusing on the tremendous difficulties before him and becoming anxious and discouraged about what to do, Jehoshaphat focused on the One whose love and power could conquer. When we look at it from God's perspective, difficulties appear in a new light. When we consciously think about God's character—His love, power, creativity, and resourcefulness—we place ourselves in a position in which we are able to receive His blessings. As we remind God (and ourselves) of the wonderful things He has done for us in the past, we create opportunities for Him to work in the future. This type of prayer also bonds us to God as we express adoration for Him.[5] Our prayers are infused with reverence, admiration, courage, and new spiritual life. No longer are our problems the center of our prayers; God is. Such prayer does not bring God down to us but instead lifts us up into His presence. In the powerful words of Ellen White, "Prayer does not change our Heavenly Father, but prayer does change our relations to him. We are thus brought nigh to God, and are enabled to unite our finite strength to his Infinite power. God grant that we may, by simple faith, take hold of his arm of strength and mercy, and receive his greatest blessings. He is the source of all good."[6]

Prayer that focuses on God's love, holiness, and power will allow us to become more honest with ourselves and with God. In the light of His compassion and perfection, we begin to see ourselves and others, our needs and desires, and our dreams and goals much differently. In this way, prayer can become a premier expression of our love for God!

But why should God even answer our prayers? When we approach

Him in prayer, we must remember that we have no résumé to recommend us. We have no track record of impressive accomplishments. We don't have exemplary love or wisdom to prove our worthiness. We have nothing with which to place God in our debt or obligate His favor. Like the poor tax collector who was too ashamed to lift his eyes to heaven, all we can do is come to God and cry out, "God, be merciful to me a sinner!" (Luke 18:13).

God knows that we are unworthy. So why does He answer our prayers? The answer is simple, "God is his own reason for answering. Prayer finds its hope not in the qualifications of the one praying, but in the character and plan of the God who is hearing."[7] God answers prayer because He is love, and He tenderly loves us. Because God is God, He delights to give good gifts to His children, doing "exceedingly abundantly above all that we ask or think" (Ephesians 3:20).

God, first and foremost, grants us the blessing of His presence. In the context of that relationship, He delights when we ask great things of Him. Such a prayer relationship can only flourish with adequate time, but most people have an instant prayer mentality. Our culture does not support a pace of life that lends itself to patient prayer. Patient prayer requires slowing down long enough to pray regularly and thoroughly, but it also means learning to wait for answers.[8]

Virtuous praying is more like cooking in a Crock-Pot rather than using a microwave or going through the McDonald's drive-through. Modern conveniences have programmed us to expect instant gratification. It's easy to want our prayers answered in mere seconds: "Give me patience, Lord. And please give me patience right now!" we whine. While God listens to our hurried and often selfish "McPrayers," they will do little to nourish our spiritual lives or to prepare our hearts to receive His will. Hasty prayers can never have the profound impact that comes through perseverance in prayer.

Jesus did not live in a fast-paced culture like ours, but He faced an even more significant time challenge: He had only three short years to complete His mission of salvation. This short time to minister meant that many people in Jesus' time would not be healed, taught, and discipled. Nevertheless, at the end of His life, Jesus could still declare, "It is finished." While perhaps He did not accomplish all He *could have* or all He *wanted to*, He nevertheless accomplished all He *needed to* because He walked in the Father's will.

Prayer helped Jesus to discern His priorities. In the quiet moments of communion with His Father, He received wisdom for what to tackle and what to leave undone. We can also receive this wisdom as we commune with our Creator. By surrendering our plans and priorities to God, our lives will become more useful, and our hearts will feel more peace.[9]

Prayer is a blessing you don't want to miss out on. This simple practice will have a profound impact on your own existence and on the well-being of others. Through prayer and thanksgiving, you can receive the assurance of God's love, the courage to persevere, the power to overcome, wisdom to discern, and peace to guard your heart and mind. Prayer will usher you into the very presence of God, which is the most valuable place a human being can ever be: "In Your presence is fullness of joy; at Your right hand are pleasures forevermore" (Psalm 16:11).

Reflection questions

1. How does prayer lift us up to God?
2. What is the benefit of praising God and recounting His blessings before we bring our requests to Him?
3. What are the dangers of vending machine/instant gratification prayers? How can we avoid falling into this trap?
4. How does it make you feel to realize that God delights in hearing and answering your prayers?

1. Ellen G. White, *Steps to Christ* (Mountain View, CA: Pacific Press®, 1956), 93.

2. For this and many other practical prayer ideas, see my book *Longing for God: A Prayer and Bible Journal* (Nampa, ID: Pacific Press®, 2017), 121–24; but particularly the important prerequisite on "Prayer That Pleases God," 43–45. For Bible-based prayers for others, see the sections titled "Suggestions for Praying Together," 280–283; "Prayers for Missionaries," 306–309; and "Suggestions for Intercession," 332–335.

3. The story is recounted in Helmut Thielicke, *The Waiting Father: Sermons on the Parables of Jesus* (Cambridge: The Lutherworth Press, 1959), 189, 190.

4. Cf. the discussion in the chapter "Prayer That Pleases God" in my book *Longing for God,* 42–45.

5. For a practical suggestion of how we can praise God in prayer, see the chapter "Praising God" in my book *Longing for God,* 94–97.

6. Ellen G. White, *Review and Herald,* May 25, 1876, 162, par. 8.

7. Paul David Tripp, *A Shelter in the Time of Storm: Meditations on God and Trouble* (Wheaton, IL: Crossway Books, 2009), 53.

8. For some reflections of what it means to wait, see chapter 3 in this book.

9. For an excellent sermon on how to follow Christ's example of time management, I recommend "The Tyranny of the Urgent: When Your Best Is Not Enough," by Mark Finley, AudioVerse, accessed November 7, 2019, https://www.audioverse.org/english/sermons /recordings/17049/the-tyranny-of-the-urgent-when-your-best-is-not-enough.html.

Chapter 8

Praying for the Unvirtuous

While others are congratulating themselves, I have to lie humbly at the foot of Christ's cross, and marvel that I am saved at all.

—Charles Spurgeon

Do you have a difficult person in your life? Most all of us do. It could be a lazy coworker, a critical boss, a nagging spouse, a rebellious child, a controlling parent, an unreliable friend, an envious enemy, or even a dear church member who consistently gets on your last nerve. Indeed, some of our fellow human beings are quite difficult to get along with. Since this is true, the question becomes: *What do we do when trying to coexist with difficult people?*

If you're like me, you start out by believing that with a little divine help, you can solve the problem. So you pray.[1] *Certainly, God is capable of helping this person realize what's wrong with them,* you think. Next, you attempt to win the person with kindness. You are patient with them, very patient indeed. You try to make subtle hints that will encourage them to change for the better. And of course, you keep praying, but nothing changes.

Finally, you decide to address the issue face to face. You gather your courage, prepare your thoughts, and carefully approach the difficult person. You are honest, candid, and as kind as possible. *Most individuals are reasonable beings,* you think. *Once I explain the problem clearly, this person should be able to understand and change.* But your efforts do not seem to produce the desired result.

Over time, you realize that it's hopeless to try to change this person.

No matter what you do, he or she will continue to disturb your peace. No matter how smoothly the rest of your life may go, unless something changes *in you,* your happiness will still depend to a large degree upon the person with whom you need to get along. Even if all your circumstances change for the better and you win the lottery, your spouse will still be grouchy, your mother-in-law will still be difficult to please, your children will still not pick up after themselves, or whoever it is, he or she will still not change.

When your efforts to improve or help someone have failed, you may be able to better understand how God must feel when He deals with us human beings. Not only does God see all the difficult people *you* have to deal with on a daily basis, but He also sees an additional person who is equally human and flawed. This additional person is *you.*

Although this awareness is difficult to accept, being honest with yourself about your own flaws can make it easier for you to relate to difficult people. You need to recognize that you are the very same kind of person that you bemoan in others. You, too, need God's forgiveness. You, too, have rather problematic character qualities that other people wish they could change.

It may be challenging for you to perceive yourself as a difficult person, but we all tend to see our own deficits and mistakes as less severe than others do. Scripture teaches that "all our righteousnesses are like filthy rags" (Isaiah 64:6). This means that despite our best attempts to live virtuously, our efforts fall short. Even our strongest virtues are not entirely free from the selfishness of sin and need the cleansing of God's forgiving grace. Our mistakes and flaws will some-times cause inconvenience and pain to others—especially to God.

Despite all the power He possesses, it is impossible for God to change you if *you* are not willing to change. This is true for every person. God woos and pursues us in His great and tender love, but even His strongest love will never force us. Because God knows everything, He sees each one of our deficiencies and mistakes in sharp focus. Amazingly, He still loves us despite our brokenness. God never gives up on us or stops loving us.

God is closely and intimately connected with the inner life of every human being. His connection with each person is much stronger than any connection we could form. He desires to live in us and with us. This means that God is uniquely and very closely confronted with every evil thought we have: every impulse of hatred, envy, pride, covetousness, greed, vanity, indifference, stubbornness, and bitterness. God is pure, holy, and innocent. His Holy Spirit experiences much more pain from the weight of our sinfulness than we can experience from the mistakes of others.

This understanding can provide us with a new perspective about changing the most difficult people we will ever have to deal with: ourselves. I have come to learn that what God does *in us* is often more important than what He does *through us*. We often focus so much on what we are trying to accomplish for God that we forget that His primary objective is to accomplish something *in us*.

God wants to develop His virtues in us, forming us into His image as we run the race He sets out for us. Sometimes we get tired of the race and start comparing ourselves with others who seem to have easier races to run. But what if the unique trials and difficulties we experience are the very things God wants to use to help us become more like Him and to protect and prepare us for future challenges? What if the "annoying" people we wish we could avoid are the very people God is trying to use to help us become more like Him?

Character development is the process through which we allow the Holy Spirit to grow God's virtues in our lives. This process takes time. It often takes longer than we think should be necessary. But we must be patient with the process. Being patient with our own growth in grace is essential if we wish to be patient with others. As we think of the patience and forgiveness God has shown us in our slow growth process, it will be easier to extend patience and forgiveness to the difficult people we interact with.

Allowing God to be the Master of all areas of our lives will lead to a gradual change in our characters. This is an ongoing process. But if we are willing to allow God to change things in our lives, He will do it. His love will impact us in such a way that we will become kinder and more courteous toward others. In His strength, we will be able to treat even the most difficult people with patience and love. Perhaps we are the only difficult people that God can change when we invite Him to do so. Or perhaps, as we allow God to change us, it will also give Him a greater opportunity to change others. Why don't you give it a try? You'll be surprised by what God can do in you and through you.

Although we can't change others directly, the Bible still encourages us to pray for them (Ephesians 6:18; 1 Timothy 2:1–3; Jeremiah 29:7).[2] These prayers will create opportunities for God to move and act in special ways. Since the Fall, we live in enemy territory. Satan is the ruler of this world (Ephesians 2:2). For this reason, our prayers make it possible for God to access and influence others in ways He would not be able to if we did not pray. While the Holy Spirit tirelessly works on every human being, God wants us to assist Him in the work as "fellow workers" (1 Corinthians 3:9) in the plan of salvation.

When we pray for others, we give God an opportunity to become active on our behalf. We can pray for our Christian brothers and sisters who need encouragement and guidance. We can pray for the people in our lives who have never experienced the living God personally. We can pray for those we know who are being damaged by the enemy's lies. And we can pray for the difficult people in our lives, not only that God will bless them, but also that He will help us to see them (and ourselves) through His eyes of love.

Reflection questions

1. What areas in your life does God need to change?
2. How does praying allow God to be active on our behalf?
3. Ask God to reveal any area where you might be a hindrance for others to clearly see the love of God and ask God to help you become more like Jesus in those areas.
4. Are you so impatient with changing the future that you are neglecting to live today to its fullest? What specific steps can you take to better engage with the present?
5. What keeps you from thanking God for those difficult people in your life that He can use to let you grow virtues in areas of your character that you otherwise might not develop?

---

1. My thoughts for this chapter have been inspired by a C. S. Lewis article, "The Trouble With . . . ," in Walter Hooper, ed., *God in the Dock: Essays on Theology and Ethics* (Grand Rapids, MI: Eerdmans, 1970), 151–155.

2. Some practical suggestions on how to pray for other people and with other people can be found in my book *Longing for God*, especially 148–152; 280–283; 306–309; 332–351.

Chapter 9

Virtuous Living Through Suffering and Loss

The darker the night, the brighter the stars.
The deeper the grief, the closer is God.

—Fyodor Dostoyevsky

Ten years ago, I lost a treasure. It wasn't a monetary treasure, although I wish it could have been. It wasn't the loss of a professional goal or personal ambition, which—although disappointing—would have been much easier to accept. But in 2009, I lost one of the most valuable treasures I've ever had—my wife, Ulrike, died of cancer. Proverbs 31 describes the value of a faithful woman,

Who can find a virtuous wife?
For her worth is far above rubies.
The heart of her husband safely trusts her;
So he will have no lack of gain (Proverbs 31:10, 11).

This passage describes Ulrike so well. Losing her was by far the most difficult thing I have ever experienced.

Grief and loss are devastating—both emotionally and spiritually.

We would like to believe that our lives are relatively stable, assuming that the blessings we experience (including the people) will remain constant. But all too often, we are jolted back to the painful reality of living in a broken world. Our faith in God's love for us can easily be shaken through suffering—especially losing a loved one.

So how do we live virtuous lives in the midst of suffering and loss? How do we cope with intense pain and unanswered questions about why God allowed a loss to occur? How do we deal with well-meaning people who try to encourage us with such trite or insensitive platitudes as God has a reason for everything, God knows best, or at least you didn't lose your entire family?

Although suffering and loss are extremely difficult, I have personally found that God comes very close during these times. He gently walks with us through "the valley of the shadow of death" (Psalm 23:4), supporting and sustaining us with His promises and provisions. Seasons of grief provide unique opportunities for us to practice virtuous living, trusting God's promise that He will never leave us or forsake us (Hebrews 13:5).

It seems that the most beautiful and the most painful experiences in life cannot be adequately described with words. How do you explain to a person who has never fallen in love what it feels like to be deeply in love? Likewise, how do you describe the loss of a loved one to someone who never knew that person? Every loss in life is unique because every person and relationship is irreplaceable. To lose a parent is different than losing a spouse. To lose a child is different than losing a friend. Yet grief cannot be quantified or measured, and it is certainly no respecter of persons.

It is also true that different people experience the pain of loss differently. Even members of the same family often have very different needs when journeying through grief. Given the complex nature of loss, it's impossible for me to provide a comprehensive list of answers to the many difficult questions that arise. Nevertheless, I *can* share a small part of my own story in the hope that it will encourage others who are experiencing the pain of suffering or loss.

I was blessed with a very happy childhood and raised by parents who believed in God and practiced their faith actively and authentically. They trained me well, but once I was old enough to think for myself, I still had to face some existential questions (including questions about God and faith) that defied easy answers. Thankfully, God continued to reveal Himself to me, and I chose to keep trusting Him.

For many years, I was not personally confronted with severe suffering or death. Perhaps as "enlightened" citizens of the Western world, living in the twenty-first century with its amazing progress in science and medicine, we have tried to forget the fact that life is fragile—that suffering, pain, sickness, and death still exist. It's easy to talk and think of death in an abstract and theoretical manner until you are confronted with it personally.

Ulrike was only forty-three years old when she was diagnosed with the most aggressive form of breast cancer. She didn't have a choice in the matter; none of us did. Ulrike still had a bright future ahead of her and was still very much needed. After staying at home with our three sons for several years, she had recently started working again as an elementary school teacher—a profession she loved. She had a gift for teaching and was well-loved and respected by both the children and her peers. She was also loved and adored in our family.

Soon after the news of her sickness spread through our community, we were bombarded by well-meaning people who claimed to know of special cures and treatments that could defy the prognosis and restore Ulrike's health. We tried everything that seemed safe and logical to try, but still the disease progressed. My wife was exemplary in her healthy lifestyle and positive and hopeful in her walk with God.

We supported her as best as we could. We prayed as we had never prayed before. Many people were praying for her. Ulrike received a special anointing for the sickness two times—once at the beginning of her illness and again toward the end, but nothing helped! She died less than a year after her diagnosis.

Those who knew Ulrike can testify that she left an amazing example of faithful living and unwavering trust in God. When she died, she was at peace with herself and with God. For her, death was a release from suffering. For our family, it was (and still is) a very harsh loss. She had accepted her death, but we still had to accept life without her.

The loss of my wife robbed my children and me of experiences that can never be recovered. We missed her loving presence at my oldest son's recent wedding. She will never have the joy of one day holding a grandchild in her arms. We can no longer share with her what we are experiencing. We miss her counsel and support. The loss is extremely painful and cannot be compensated with anything. Sometimes people say that time heals all wounds. That's not true. Time itself can be the wound. Even though the initial pain of Ulrike's loss has grown less intense with the passing of time, some of our memories of her have also faded away, causing a different type of loss. Her absence remains a sore spot in our lives.

Suffering is perhaps one of the most acute temptations of faith. The pain of suffering raises tenacious and troubling questions about God that are difficult to answer. The doubt that suffering initiates has a strong potential to destroy our faith.[1] All of a sudden, traditional explanations and answers to suffering no longer make sense. Instead, we are confronted with haunting "why" questions.

I am familiar with these questions. Loss feels so senseless that it's only natural to ask why: Why us? Why her? Why now? In order to cope with this, we decided to raise an alternate set of "why" questions: Why should sickness, suffering, and death affect others, but *not* us? we asked. After all, we live in a sinful and imperfect world. Christians are promised eternal life but are not exempt from sickness and death on this side of eternity.

If we follow God only to be spared from suffering and death, we follow Him for the wrong reasons! As virtuous children of God, we can live our lives (even when facing adversity) in such a way that others will not doubt God's goodness to us, but instead, see it revealed through our faith. The Bible instructs us how to grieve in a way that keeps our faith intact. Paul wrote that we do not "sorrow as others who have no hope" (1 Thessalonians 4:13). Our hope in God's promises can have a contagious effect on the people who observe us during suffering and loss.

Life raises certain questions that cannot be explained theoretically but are only answered *experientially* as we live in faith, allowing God's grace and goodness to become visible in our lives. God certainly finds no pleasure in sickness and death. Only the devil enjoys watching us suffer. In an attempt to shipwreck our faith, he tempts us to doubt God's goodness. Although we suffered tremendously, my family and I firmly decided not to grant the enemy this pleasure.

To suffer is difficult enough, but to suffer without meaning feels unbearable. And yet, life often presents us with painful situations for which we do not have adequate explanations. In these times, I have desperately wanted to find or construct reasons for what I am experiencing so that my suffering will not be meaningless. Nonetheless, I've learned to live with some unanswered questions—trusting that even though I don't understand, there is One who knows all things and is constantly working for my good.

Although I don't fully understand why God allowed my wife to die rather than intervening for her healing, I want my life to show that I still trust His goodness. He sees the big picture and is constantly working for the well-being of His children. Regardless of what we experience, we can "trust everything to the hand that was nailed to the cross for us."[2]

When going through adversity, it's easy to hope that our circumstances will change. We desperately hope that our losses will be prevented, our conflicts will disappear, and our inconveniences will simply go away. We also start comparing ourselves with others—envying those who seemingly have less to suffer or more to enjoy than we do.[3]

By focusing on the difficulties and obstacles, or ruminating on the unfairness of life, we can easily lose our focus on God, who alone is the foundation and surety of our hope. I have learned through my experience that situations like this confront me with crucial decisions. Will I question God's goodness and power because of my pain, or will I accept each life experience as a unique opportunity to draw closer to Him and to become the person He wants me to be? Will I believe the promise of Scripture that "all things work together for good to those who love God" (Romans 8:28), trusting that He can bring blessing out of even the most painful circumstances?

I still distinctly remember the moment when I realized what this meant for me. I had to ask myself the very difficult question: Was I really willing to accept that the loss of my wife was now part of my life? This was not planned. This was not my fault. This was not fair. This was not how I had envisioned my future. Yet it was part of my life. The tremendous loss had become part of my biography, distinguishing me from the person I was before. Whether I wanted to admit it or not, it was part of my new identity.

Despite these realizations, accepting this was not easy for me. I was tempted to remain in an illusory state of mind, a make-believe world in which I would not allow the reality of her loss to be part of my life. It seemed far easier to repress the pain than to acknowledge and accept it, but God gave me courage to confront the mechanisms of my denial and to face the painful reality of Ulrike's absence with all that it meant. Only as I did this was I able to start cautiously ordering my everyday life without her.

When I gave up my inner resistance to accepting life without Ulrike, I cried many tears of grief and pain. At the same time, I felt as if a heavy load was lifted off my shoulders. It was as if God lifted me up and gave me wings to help me soar like the eagles again. My decision to accept the loss did not answer every question I had. Loss is a learning process that sometimes lasts for a lifetime.

In my book *Longing for God*, I share practical things that helped me cope with my loss, keeping me spiritually sane and even joyful. I especially recommend the simple exercise to develop an attitude of gratitude, and the suggestions on how to pray meaningfully for others. These practices have opened up new horizons in my personal walk with God.[4]

Of course, as a single parent and man, I have special needs and longings that cannot be easily stilled. The enemy always presents temptations for us to numb our pain and loneliness with things that bring quick pleasure but no lasting satisfaction or joy. I have learned—and am still learning—what it means to trust God day by day and to live by faith.

To live by faith is easily said, but I won't be able to succeed if I try to fabricate solutions to my own problems on my own terms. Instead, I must learn in every area of life to trust God and His amazing grace, even when I don't see how He will ever be able to meet my needs. Then again, I must remember that God has "a thousand ways to provide for us of which we know nothing"[5] (cf. Jeremiah 33:3). This beautiful truth is something that I cannot adequately express in words but have repeatedly experienced in my own life. To trust God's grace and goodness, remaining connected with Him in difficult times, is worth all the effort it requires. We have a compassionate Father who wants us to bring our longings to Him.

Longing, to me, is a remarkably delightful word. It seems that human beings are never more human than when they are longing for someone or something, with a sparkle and fire in their eyes. To be human is to be full of expectation.

The Christian who longs is not ultimately satisfied with things as they are but still chooses to remain content and grateful, trusting in God's goodness despite pain and suffering. I long to see the day when Jesus will come again, when God's great love ultimately proves stronger than even death, resurrecting those who have trusted in Him! Then God will wipe away every tear from our eyes, and "there shall be no more death, nor sorrow, nor crying. There shall be no more pain" (Revelation 21:4).

Reflection questions

1. How can changing the "Why me?" question to "Why not me?" alter our attitude toward suffering?
2. How can suffering and loss become unique opportunities to draw closer to God?
3. How does focusing on God's goodness help us in times of suffering?
4. God promises to one day wipe away all tears. What does this promise mean to you personally?

---

1. Paul David Tripp has written an insightful book about the experience of suffering, when life does not make sense anymore. If you want to learn more about various challenges posed by the human experience of suffering and how to deal with them from a spiritual perspective, I recommend the following books by Paul David Tripp: *Suffering: Gospel Hope When Life Doesn't Make Sense* (Wheaton, IL: Crossway, 2018) and his remarkable and encouraging book *A Shelter in the Time of Storm* (Wheaton, IL: Crossway, 2009).

2. Ellen G. White, *Steps to Christ* (Mountain View, CA: Pacific Press®, 1956), 103.

3. See my thoughts on envy, the enemy of virtue, in chapter 4 of this book.

4. Frank M. Hasel, *Longing for God: A Prayer and Bible Journal* (Nampa, ID: Pacific Press®, 2017).

5. Ellen G. White, *The Ministry of Healing* (Nampa, ID: Pacific Press®, 2003), 481.

Chapter 10

The Virtue of Digital Detox

Make time for the quiet moments,
as God whispers and the world is loud.

—Unknown

A friend of mine is in a toxic relationship. He spends an inordinate amount of time with his partner, failing to invest in other areas of life. He's so dependent that he gets very anxious if left alone for more than a few minutes. He can't seem to make decisions without consulting his lover, who expects many hours of his time each day—constantly distracting him, following him everywhere he goes, and even distancing him from his friends. He realizes his partner is needy and demanding but can't seem to set proper boundaries. Perhaps the saddest part of the story is that my friend isn't dating a woman. He's simply in a relationship with his phone.

We live in extraordinary times. Technology has fundamentally changed the way we live, work, think, and communicate. Technology can be a blessing—connecting us with faraway friends, supplying valuable information, and providing new tools for Bible study and evangelism. But technology also comes with very real temptations and risks.

The digital age is marked by a strange paradox—although it connects us with infinite possibilities, it can easily isolate us from real-life relationships. It can also keep us so distracted that we miss out on what matters the most. Virtual reality—as real as it may seem—is a far cry from life in the real world. If we're not careful, our virtual living may compete with our virtuous living.

Virtues are not created instantaneously or in the digital realm—they grow only through real-life experiences. Virtuous living requires quiet, uninterrupted time to pray, meditation on God's Word, and thoughtful evaluation of our lives. Virtual distractions can easily intrude upon this time. To protect ourselves from this, we must be mindful and intentional about the way we manage time and use technology.

Staring at a screen

While recently dining at a restaurant, I noticed that every other customer in sight was on his or her smartphone. As I rode a city bus in Europe, I noticed that hardly any of the passengers made eye contact. Instead, they stared at their smartphones, continuing to stare even as they left the bus and walked into traffic! Smartphones can be so alluring that we allow them to isolate us and even compromise our safety.

Technology gives us an illusion of self-dependence. We don't need to ask for directions anymore; we have apps that will guide us. We don't need to discuss different opinions with colleagues and friends; that's what Google is for. With a few simple clicks and swipes, we can roam the whole world and have access to more information than we could absorb in a lifetime.

Information overload

The nearly infinite amount of information at our fingertips poses each one of us a serious challenge: How do I find my way in the digital data jungle? What data is preselected for me by algorithms (and marketing ploys) rather than a wise selection of the content I need? How can I trust the selection of choices that Google and other search engines make for me?

In previous generations, a lack of access to information could seriously handicap a person's knowledge and well-being. Today, we have the opposite challenge—navigating through a maze of endlessly available information. Often, we are left overloaded and just as ill informed as when we began—but with the illusion that *we now know.*

The data

Technology promises freedom but can easily take us captive. Much of technology, particularly social media, has been deliberately engineered for addiction. Once we're accustomed to it, it's hard to live without. Consider these sobering statistics.[1]

- We check our smartphones every 4.3 minutes of our waking lives.
- The average American spends 30 percent of leisure time online.
- Fifty percent of people prefer to communicate digitally rather than in person.
- Sixty-one percent admit to being addicted to their devices and the internet.
- The average employee checks forty websites a day, switching activities thirty-seven times an hour (more than once every two minutes). Only an estimated 2 percent of people can multitask without a decline in performance.
- Thirty-three percent of people admit to hiding from family and friends to check social media.
- Ninety-five percent of people use electronics in the hour leading up to bed. Artificial screen light can decrease melatonin production and interfere with sleep.
- Unplugging for just one day gives some users mental and physical withdrawal symptoms.
- Ninety-five percent of American teens have access to a smartphone, and 45 percent say they are online almost constantly.[2]

The statistics are similar in many other countries around the world.

A new moral compass

Whatever we trust the most inevitably becomes our moral compass. Social media and popular culture have created a standard of "virtuous living" that often does not align with Scripture. Politically correct beliefs are promoted with almost religious overtones. People are publicly humiliated when they fail to reach the ever-changing standard. We all crave approval and respect. Sadly, the enemy has taken advantage of this on social media, leading people to adopt the culture's values rather than God's values. We need to be mindful of our own vulnerability to being negatively influenced in this way.

Opportunity cost

In economics, the term *opportunity cost* refers to the valuable thing a person will miss out on if they invest a resource in something else. For example, if you spend money buying a new car, you will not be able to use that same money to pay for a trip to Europe, a down payment on your house, and so on.

Every choice you make has an opportunity cost. If you stay up too late, you'll pay the opportunity cost of sleep. If you're a workaholic, you'll pay the opportunity cost of social connection. And if you heavily invest in virtual reality, your real-life reality will pay the price.

The cumulative time the average person spends online is astounding. Some unique tools have been developed to show the opportunity cost of this time: how many books a person could read, how much exercise they could get, how much more money they could make, and so on, if they invested in these things rather than excessive screen time. Benjamin Franklin once said, "Beware of little expenses; a small leak will sink a great ship."[3] Excessive screen time creates a "small leak" in our daily lives that ends up draining us of long-term effectiveness and happiness.

As Christians, the opportunity cost of our digital habits is especially high. The overuse of technology can literally erode our relationships with God and others.[4] Many Christians walk more closely with their smartphones than with God. Each day, God has valuable lessons for us to learn, gifts for us to enjoy, relationships for us to experience, and goals for us to accomplish. The choices we make each day have long-term and even *eternal* consequences for both ourselves and others. As we interact with technology, let's remember that how we spend our hours is how we spend our days and how we spend our days, of course, is how we spend our lives.

Creating a margin

Each one of us needs a margin of time and space in our lives to protect our well-being. Technology threatens this margin. It has been pointed out that "technological progress inevitably complicates life as it adds both to our responsibilities and to our choices for information and entertainment. Economic progress rarely results in more leisure; rather, it typically leads to more work and more debt, which leads to more pressure to work."[5]

Constant overstimulation depletes our reserves and does not allow us an adequate margin in the use of our bodies, emotions, money, and time. This leads to diminished energy, burnout, and even collapse. Many of us desperately need to simplify our lives in order to enjoy the beauty of real life again. The virtue of fasting can be a helpful step in the right direction.

Another kind of fast

There are many things we need to unlearn in order to renew our appreciation for real-life experiences. We need to deliberately disengage from things that clutter our time, compromise our health and relationships, and poison our spiritual growth. We need to disconnect in order to reconnect with real life and with God.[6] We need to digitally detox.[7]

Here we can learn from biblical men and women of faith who, when they realized their need to reconnect with God, made it a priority by fasting (Esther 4:3; 2 Chronicles 20:3; Daniel 9:3; Acts 13:2, 3). Fasting is the deliberate choice to abstain from something that is available to me but that might distract me from God. By declaring a "time-out" on whatever is absorbing my time, energy, and attention, I can seek God and listen to Him in a focused and unhurried way.

Through fasting, I consciously set aside undisturbed time for God that would otherwise be filled with mundane things. My vision turns from my daily routine to things of eternal significance. By abstaining from something I use on a daily basis, I acknowledge that I do not live by bread alone (nor by the internet alone) but by "every word that comes from the mouth of God" (Matthew 4:4, NIV). As such, fasting should not "be confined to the question of food and drink; fasting should really be made to include abstinence from anything which is legitimate in and of itself for the sake of some special spiritual purpose."[8]

Would you like to experience the benefit of fasting? Try taking a scheduled break from television, the internet, email, social media, your smartphone, or some other distraction in order to reconnect with God, yourself, and others. Fasting is less about giving something up and more about choosing something better. Below are a few ideas that can help you digitally detox.

The digital detox diet

1. In the morning, go online only after you have spent time with God and His Word and decided what you need to do that day. In this way, you and God can determine your agenda together before you get derailed by urgent emails, social media, the news, and so on.

2. Twice a day, work for one hour offline. Put your phone on airplane mode and turn your internet connection off. After some practice, you will be amazed at how productive you are.

3. Consider setting aside a half or full day once or twice each month to deliberately disconnect and focus instead on what is important to you spiritually, professionally, and personally.

4. Check your emails only during restricted periods during the day. Keep your email inbox notifications turned off during the rest of the day—even on your smartphone.

5. In the hour before you go to sleep, turn off your devices and read a good book. Why not the Bible?

6. Use an app or phone feature to track and record your screen time each week, and/or to limit your use of certain social media platforms. Pay attention to the cumulative time you are spending and set goals for the amount of time you want to spend.

7. Have you thought about Sabbath rest from your digital world? Leave your phone on flight mode (or at home) and leave your computer off during the Sabbath hours. This will enable you to enjoy quality time with your Creator and Redeemer, as well as with the valuable people He has placed in your life.[9]

I will leave you with an amazing insight from a Christian writer that I greatly admire. She wrote the following words long before there was even such a thing as the internet or the temptations of the digital world as we face them today. And yet, her timeless wisdom shines brightly when she writes,

An intensity such as never before was seen is taking possession of the world. In amusement, in moneymaking, in the contest for power, in the very struggle for existence, there is a terrible force that engrosses body and mind and soul. In the midst of this maddening rush, God is speaking. He bids us come apart and commune with Him. "Be still, and know that I am God." Psalm 46:10.

Many, even in their seasons of devotion, fail of receiving the blessing of real communion with God. They are in too great haste. With hurried steps they press through the circle of Christ's loving presence, pausing perhaps a moment within the sacred precincts, but not waiting for counsel. They have no time to remain with the divine Teacher. With their burdens they return to their work.

These workers can never attain the highest success until they learn the secret of strength. They must give themselves time to think, to pray, to wait upon God for a renewal of physical, mental, and spiritual power. They need the uplifting influence of His Spirit. Receiving this, they will be quickened by fresh life. The wearied frame and tired brain will be refreshed, the burdened heart will be lightened.[10]

May this be our experience, I pray.

Reflection questions

1. How much time do you spend each day or week on your smartphone or other devices?
2. What is your default means of communication with friends and family?
3. What is the ratio of your screen time to time with God? How do you feel about this balance?
4. Try a digital detox and reflect on how it impacts your priorities.

---

1. Except as otherwise noted, the subsequent statistics have been drawn from Digital Detox, accessed July 22, 2019, http://digitaldetox.org; and from the engaging book by Tony Reinke, *12 Ways Your Phone Is Changing You* (Wheaton, IL: Crossway, 2017).

2. Monica Anderson and Jingjing Jiang, "Teens, Social Media & Technology 2018," Pew Research Center, May 31, 2018 (accessed August 23, 2019), https://www.pewinternet.org /2018/05/31/teens-social-media-technology-2018/.

3. Benjamin Franklin, *Poor Richard's Almanac: Selections From the Apothegms and Proverbs, With a Brief Sketch of the Life of Benjamin Franklin* (Waterloo, IA: U.S.C. Publishing, 1914), 16.

4. Donald S. Whitney, *Simplify Your Spiritual Life: Spiritual Disciplines for the Overwhelmed* (Colorado Springs, CO: NavPress, 2003), 171.

5. Whitney, *Simplify Your Spiritual Life*, 171.

6. Cf. Tony Reinke, *12 Ways Your Phone is Changing You*, and more recently, Tony Reinke, *Competing Spectacles: Treasuring Christ in the Media Age* (Wheaton, IL: Crossways, 2019).

7. See Digital Detox, accessed July 30, 2019, http://digitaldetox.org.

8. Martyn Lloyd-Jones, *Studies in the Sermon of the Mount*, vol. 2 (Grand Rapids, MI: Eerdmans, 1960), 38, as quoted in John Piper, *A Hunger for God: Desiring God Through Fasting and Prayer* (Wheaton, IL: Crossway Books, 1997), 200.

9. For more thoughts on the virtue of keeping the Sabbath holy, see chapter 11 in this book.

10. Ellen G. White, *Education* (Nampa, ID: Pacific Press®, 2002), 260, 261.

Chapter 11

The Virtuous Rest

Come to me, all you who are weary and burdened,
and I will give you rest.
—Jesus, Matthew 11:28, NIV

If you watch your step on the Sabbath and don't use my
holy day for personal advantage, if you treat the Sabbath as
a day of joy, GOD's holy day as a celebration, if you honor it
by refusing "business as usual," making money, running here
and there—then you'll be free to enjoy GOD!
—Isaiah 58:13, 14, *The Message*

One of the best-kept secrets of virtuous living is the observance of Sabbath rest. This ancient spiritual practice brings incredible riches on its wings—riches that wait to be rediscovered. The unique discipline of Sabbath observance provides many profound blessings—forming us spiritually, restoring our energy, enhancing our relationships, and increasing our enjoyment of the beauty of God and His creation.

Our 24/7 culture moves at hyperspeed, honoring busyness over balance and consumerism over connection. For many people, rest and peace are elusive, but like a breath of fresh air, the Sabbath can liberate us from the stifling effects of overwork, consumerism, and the anxiety of self-dependence. It opens up a liberating new perspective that enriches our lives far more than the accumulation of more and more material things.

This might come as a surprise to many readers because the Sabbath is often misunderstood. Some Christians wonder why it should be kept at all, while others experience it as a legalistic burden rather than a spiritual delight.[1] The apostle Paul instructs us, "Discipline yourself for the purpose of godliness" (1 Timothy 4:7, NASB). The Sabbath actually can be a very practical way of fleshing out this command of the apostle Paul that calls us to practice virtuous living. The Sabbath, appreciated as a spiritual discipline, can help us focus on the right things, including the most important of all: knowing God and following His healing will for our lives. Rightly practiced, the Sabbath will bring some simplicity and order to our hectic daily work, and it will lead us to become more like Jesus. It can also help prevent some destructive habits. This chapter will briefly explore the Sabbath's unique ability to enhance the way we live, think, and walk with God.[2]

The origin of the Sabbath

In order to understand the true value of the Sabbath, we briefly need to go back to Scripture. In our modern world, the meaning of the seventh day has become a "theological orphan" because we have lost touch with the biblical text.[3] Many people view the Sabbath as an isolated or outdated doctrine, failing to see its vital role in the process of salvation and the practice of Christian virtue.

The Sabbath was one of the crowning acts of Creation. For six days, God's infinite love was manifested through Christ's creative power.[4] In Exodus 20:11, we are told that "in six days the LORD made heaven and earth, the sea, and all that is in them, and rested on the seventh day. Therefore, the LORD blessed the Sabbath day and made it holy" (ESV). At the beginning of human life, God gave us this example. On the seventh day, "he rested and was refreshed" (Exodus 31:17, ESV). God didn't just command Sabbath observance; He set a personal example for us to follow. Humans are invited to imitate their Maker by joining the rhythm of time established at Creation. As beings created in God's image, we can become more like Him by observing this special day.

Many people believe that the Sabbath is a Jewish custom, but this gift of time reaches all the way back to Creation—long before the formation of the Jewish race. When questioned about the Sabbath, Jesus said, "The Sabbath was made for man [*anthropos*], and not man for the Sabbath" (Mark 2:27). The Greek word *anthropos* refers to all humankind, not to a specific nation or race. None of us are excluded from the gift of the Sabbath.

The Sabbath and human value

The Sabbath reminds us that we are deeply valued and loved by the God who created us. It reveals the inherent worth of every human being. According to pastor and philosopher Don Postema, the Sabbath "affirms the dignity of all people. When no one is working, it is hard to tell the difference between them by their achievements. They are equal as image-bearers of God, as persons loved by God! So Sabbath is a sign of divine grace, a reminder of who we are before God. We have value beyond what we produce or achieve. In fact, we are accepted by God before we do or achieve anything important."[5]

Adam and Eve were given the task of cultivating the exquisitely beautiful Garden of Eden. However, before they ever lifted a finger to work, they first celebrated the Sabbath—a time of delightful communion with their Creator and dearest Friend. This sequence reveals a valuable lesson: in the mind of God, our work gains its significance out of the time we have first spent with Him.

Sabbath rest, however, doesn't happen automatically. We must thoughtfully prepare and plan for it. As the Sabbath begins, heaven touches the earth with rest. Accepting the gift, we enjoy a sense of sweet relief and closure to what occupied us during the week. Nevertheless, in order for this to happen, we must *choose* to stop. We must leave unfinished work undone, distancing ourselves from the appealing opportunities and distractions that vie for our attention. Sometimes this means unplugging from technology and consciously shifting our thoughts and conversations to remain in the restful space of God's holy day. While the world around us refuses to slow down or be still, God uses the Sabbath to create a counterculture. Sabbath rest provides the margin in time we desperately need. It puts us in sync with Heaven's schedule, providing the ends and beginnings we need to flourish.

Switching cycles

Have you ever wondered why we observe the cycles of time that we do? Most cycles are straightforward. In a day, the earth rotates around its axis. In a month, the moon circles the earth. In a year, the earth travels around the sun. However, the week can't be traced to any such cycle—it has an identity all its own.

Many scientists conclude that the week was an "arbitrary construct," imposed on time by people long ago but "unrelated to anything in the natural order."[6] But if the seven-day cycle is only something that was arbitrarily imposed on time by human beings, it is remarkable that several attempts to modify this weekly cycle have miserably failed. After the French Revolution, an attempt was made to replace the seven-day week (because of its religious origin) with a secular ten-day week. Citizens worked for nine days before a day of rest was given. This experiment was short-lived, and the decision was eventually reversed.[7] In 1929, the Soviet Union attempted to replace the traditional week with a five-day week designed to make people more productive. Rather than having official days off, periods of rest were rationed on different days of the week. Stalin and his associates believed that weekend rest threatened the industrial progress of the nation, claiming that "machines need never be idle."[8] Nevertheless, this initiative also failed miserably. It led to burnout, diminished family relationships, and a lack of social cohesion.

The seven-day week was eventually reinstated.

Our loving Creator designed the seven-day cycle and the Sabbath rest for the benefit of all creation. He even commanded that animals be allowed to rest on the Sabbath (Deuteronomy 5:14). As part of God's creation, we are biologically and spiritually designed to operate on this cycle.

Remember to remember

It's ironic (and sad) that the only commandment that begins with the word *remember* is the commandment that most followers of Jesus have forgotten. I will not take time here to explain the history of man's attempt to change the seventh-day Sabbath[9] but will simply remind my readers that Scripture makes clear the enduring nature of the Sabbath. After creating the Sabbath in Eden (Genesis 2:1–3), God reminded His people of its importance by including it in the Ten Commandments given at Mount Sinai (Exodus 20:8–11). The Old Testament is filled with examples of Sabbath keeping, as well as God's pain and displeasure when the Sabbath was not observed (Exodus 16:22–29; Nehemiah 13:15–22; Isaiah 58:13, 14).

The New Testament follows this same pattern. Jesus carefully observed the Sabbath in His own life and claimed to be Lord of the Sabbath (Luke 4:16; Matthew 5:17, 18; Mark 2:28). He instructed His followers to observe the Sabbath far into the future, even after His death and resurrection (Matthew 24:20). Jesus even modeled Sabbath keeping in His own death, resting in the grave on Sabbath, and resuming His work on resurrection Sunday. (Luke 23:54–56; 24:1–7). The early Christians (both Jews and Gentiles) observed the seventh-day Sabbath (Acts 13:13–15, 42). The Bible even predicted that attempts to change the Sabbath would occur in the future and that these attempts would be motivated by the enemy of God (Daniel 7:25). The seventh-day Sabbath is as real and relevant today as it was in the Garden of Eden.

The Sabbath and freedom

The reason God asks us to *exclude* certain activities on the Sabbath is because He wants us to *include* the very *best* activities, making the day as rich as possible (cf. Isaiah 58:13, 14). According to theologian Donald Whitney, Sabbath observance helps us to restore margins in every area of our lives by "deliberately scheduling freedom *from* some things and freedom *for* some things: freedom from busy work, freedom from commerce, freedom from electronic communication and entertainment. We also need to schedule freedom for quality time with God in worship, in reading his word, the replenishment of the body in rest, and reading, and hearing, and singing, and quality time with family and friends."[10]

It is impossible to over-invest in the Sabbath. If you observe this day the way God intends, you will always get more out of it than you put in. Perhaps this is what Jesus meant when He said, "The Sabbath was made for man, and not man for the Sabbath" (Mark 2:27). When we offer God our worship and adoration through Sabbath observance, we open a channel through which He can bless and refresh us abundantly. Enjoying nature on the Sabbath can provide just such a glimpse into God's generous and loving heart. " 'God is love' is written upon every opening bud, upon every spire of springing grass. The lovely birds making the air vocal with their happy songs, the delicately tinted flowers in their perfection perfuming the air, the lofty trees of the forest with their rich foliage of living green—all testify to the tender, fatherly care of our God and to His desire to make His children happy."[11]

Service and the Sabbath

During His ministry, Jesus was accused by religious leaders who claimed He was breaking the Sabbath through His acts of healing (Matthew 12:10; Mark 3:2; John 9:14–16). The Pharisees even declared, "This Man is not from God, because He does not keep the

Sabbath" (John 9:16). On one occasion, a man with a withered hand was brought to Jesus in the synagogue. Jesus was asked, "Is it lawful to heal on the Sabbath?" The Pharisees asked this "that they might accuse Him" (Matthew 12:10).

Jesus responded by first asking a question, " 'What man is there among you who has one sheep, and if it falls into a pit on the Sabbath, will not lay hold of it and lift it out? Of how much more value then is a man than a sheep? Therefore it is lawful to do good on the Sabbath.' Then He said to the man, 'Stretch out your hand.' And he stretched it out, and it was restored as whole as the other. Then the Pharisees went out and plotted against Him, how they might destroy Him" (Matthew 12:11–14).

Jesus healed this man at great personal risk, clearly demonstrating that God delights to relieve suffering on the Sabbath. We can follow His example by taking time on the Sabbath to visit the sick, encourage the suffering, seek out the lonely, lift the burden of those who are sad and who mourn by sharing some creative gestures of friendliness, and remind those around us of God's compassion and infinite love. Each week, the Sabbath is a gentle and joyful reminder of what matters most in life: connecting with God, connecting with others, and sharing God's goodness with those who need it the most.

Being fully present on the Sabbath

The world around us rushes on at an unprecedented speed. In order to truly experience Sabbath rest, we must intentionally minimize our distractions. This requires planning ahead to complete our work before the Sabbath hours (Mark 15:42; Luke 23:54; John 19:31) and also having a plan in place to minimize the countless distractions that present themselves on the Sabbath. This may mean planning Sabbath activities ahead of time (church, fellowship, time in nature, etc.), guiding social conversations along spiritual themes, and taking a break from (or limiting) our screen time on the Sabbath.[12]

In a time when only a "few people seem to be making specific choices to put any limits on texting, social media, or other uses of digital technology, Sabbath may in fact call for some limits if we are to experience Sabbath's deepest blessings—not only on the Sabbath but on the other six days too."[13] The profound way in which digital technology is influencing our minds and our relationships with God requires more than a surface understanding. Let's take a closer look at this phenomenon and explore how Sabbath rest can offer some very practical blessings to a generation that is shaped relationally and morally by using new technology in an age of digital connectedness.[14]

The Sabbath and the digitally connected mind
Research reveals that our brains are literally rewired by the ways we engage with the internet and digital information. As we text, look up information online, and scroll through various social media platforms, our brains become accustomed to

- scanning massive amounts of information in short periods of time;
- distinguishing between what is most important and what is peripheral;
- analyzing content swiftly;
- making quick decisions (whether to keep reading or to click to the next page).

During this process, the neurons and synapses our brains use for this type of thinking grow larger and stronger, making these sorts of mental processes easier for us. Since our brains naturally like to do what they are good at, we start to crave activities that require this type of thinking (i.e., the same online activities that started the cycle).[15]

Using our brains in the manner described above can have some positive benefits,[16] but too much of this type of processing will negatively impact our patterns of thinking. Does the following scenario sound familiar? You receive a text from a friend, then decide to check his Facebook page. While there, you click on a link he posted about an interesting article, then click on a news story *that* article links to, only to be interrupted by another message on your phone, then . . .

Why is this a problem? "The type of thinking developed is scattered and shallow. Skimming media-rich web pages exposes us to large quantities of information and visuals, but the brain's ability to actually learn is diminished, and understanding is weakened. We become less able to engage in undistracted, deep thinking."[17]

This is a sobering reality. While people who frequently use the internet are spending more time reading, this type of reading is "characterized by browsing and scanning, keyword spotting, one-time reading, [and] non-linear reading . . . while less time is spent on in-depth reading and concentrated reading."[18] This change in the structure of our brains makes it physiologically more difficult to follow an extended line of thinking, to understand a nuanced description of a political conflict, or to solve problems that require multiple steps.

This fragmented style of thinking also makes it more difficult to reflect deeply on the words and ways of God:[19] "It's like trying to run a 10k race when you've mainly been using your legs to walk from the couch to the refrigerator."[20]

According to Jesus, the first and greatest commandment is to "love the LORD your God with all your heart, with all your soul, with all your *mind*" (Mark 12:30; emphasis added). For this reason, we need to pay careful attention to any habits that alter our brains and influence our thinking.[21]

Virtuous living requires a certain state of mind and quality of thought. Our spiritual growth is nurtured by times of sustained prayer, the ability to wait in undistracted silence, and the ability to contemplate and reflect on God and His Word. It has been pointed out that "these activities require us to use the parts of our brains that allow us to think calmly, to be undistracted, and to focus for extended periods of time. . . . The use of digital technology does not foster the type of thinking that develops the brain circuits needed for contemplation, undistracted prayer, and other such dimensions of spiritual formation."[22]

How the Sabbath can help

Thankfully, we can place ourselves in a more spiritual and relational state of mind by practicing digital detox and observing God's Sabbath rest. Imagine what blessings could grow out of one full day in which you turn off your devices, ignore your social media and email, and instead choose to be fully present. The Sabbath provides the perfect opportunity to enjoy quality conversations with those around you—listening attentively to their stories, enjoying nature together, and forming attachments that will enrich your life. Most important, the Sabbath invites you to reconnect with your Maker—taking unhurried time to speak with Him and to reflect creatively and deeply on His Word.

By making virtuous choices that reflect the spirit of the Sabbath, we can actually "strengthen certain parts of our brains in ways that allow us to be more focused, think more deeply, and be more compassionate at other times of the week too."[23] Sabbath observance can actually shape our neural pathways and strengthen our minds, enabling us to live more virtuously. Moreover, Scripture teaches it's impossible to live more virtuously without living *more abundantly* (James 1:25; John 10:10).

Reflection questions

1. How can the Sabbath be an antidote to the 24/7 busyness of our culture?
2. How does the Sabbath provide both endings and beginnings?

What added value does this offer to our everyday life?

3. How can you follow Jesus' example of doing good on the Sabbath?

4. Digital activity expands our brains to process vast quantities of information and to multitask. Why is the silent contemplation of God's Word necessary for virtuous living?

5. The Sabbath can restore margins in all areas of our lives. What could this look like in your life?

6. What do you think God wants to accomplish for you specifically during the coming Sabbaths?

---

1. For those who would like to further explore the meaning and blessing of Sabbath rest, the following books can give some valuable insights. A readable introduction to the legitimacy and blessing of the Sabbath can be found in Clifford Goldstein's *A Pause for Peace: What God's Gift of the Sabbath Can Mean to You* (Boise, ID: Pacific Press®, 1992); Mark Finley, *When God Said Remember* (Boise, ID: Pacific Press®, 2009); and Sigve K. Tonstad, *The Lost Meaning of the Seventh Day* (Berrien Springs, MI: Andrews University Press, 2009). For an inspiring account of the beauty and blessing of keeping the Sabbath from a Protestant perspective, see Rob Muthiah, *The Sabbath Experiment: Spiritual Formation for Living in a Non-Stop World* (Eugene, OR: Cascade Books, 2015); Marva Dawn, *Keeping the Sabbath Wholly: Ceasing, Resting, Embracing, Feasting* (Grand Rapids, MI: Eerdmans, 1989); and Walter Brueggemann, *Sabbath as Resistance: Saying No to the Culture of Now* (Louisville, KY: Westminster Press, 2017).

2. For some other aspects of the many Sabbath blessings, see my brief thoughts in the chapter 12, p. 112, 113.

3. Tonstad, *The Lost Meaning of the Seventh Day*, 21.

4. Cf. Ellen G. White, *The Desire of Ages* (Nampa, ID: Pacific Press®, 2005), 20.

5. Donald Postema, *Catch Your Breath* (Grand Rapids, MI: CRC Publications, 1997), 66, as quoted in Lynne M. Baab, *Sabbath: The Gift of Rest: 8 Studies for Individuals or Groups With Notes for Leaders*, A LifeGuide Bible Study (Downers Grove, IL: IVP Connect: An Imprint of InterVarsity Press, 2007), 16.

6. Cf. Eviatar Zerubavel, *The Seven Day Circle. The History and Meaning of the Week* (Chicago, IL: University of Chicago Press, 1989).

7. "French Republican Calendar," Encyclopaedia Britannica, accessed November 19, 2019, https://www.britannica.com/science/French-republican-calendar.

8. Natasha Frost, "For 11 Years, the Soviet Union Had No Weekends," History, last modified August 30, 2018, https://www.history.com/news/soviet-union-stalin-weekend-labor-policy.

9. On the history of man's attempt to change the seventh-day Sabbath as a day of rest, see Samuele Bacchiocchi, *From Sabbath to Sunday: A Historical Investigation of the Rise of Sunday Observance in Early Christianity* (Rome: Pontifical Gregorian University, 1977), and the chapters

on the history of the Sabbath in Kenneth A. Strand, ed., *The Sabbath in Scripture and History* (Washington, D.C.: Review and Herald®, 1982).

10. Donald S. Whitney, *Simplify Your Spiritual Life: Spiritual Disciplines for the Overwhelmed* (Colorado Springs, CO: NavPress, 2003), 171, 172.

11. Ellen G. White, *Steps to Christ* (Mountain View, CA: Pacific Press®, 1956), 10.

12. For some inspiration on how to disconnect from the influences of the digital world in order to reconnect to real life and God's reality, see chapter 10, pp. 93, 94.

13. Muthiah, *The Sabbath Experiment*, 30.

14. For some inspiration on how to disconnect from the influences of the digital world in order to reconnect to real life and God's reality, see chapter 10, pp. 93, 94.

15. Muthiah, *The Sabbath Experiment*, 32. 33.

16. Those parts of our brain that are used for fast-paced problem solving can experience a strengthening, and there can be a slight expansion of the brain's working memory capacity. It may also help older people keep their minds sharp, and it strengthens visual spatial skills (see Muthiah, *The Sabbath Experiment*, 33).

17. Muthiah, *The Sabbath Experiment*, 33.

18. According to Ziming Liu, a professor at San Jose State University, "Reading Behavior," 705, as quoted in Muthiah, *The Sabbath Experiment*, 34.

19. Muthiah, *The Sabbath Experiment*, 34.

20. Muthiah, *The Sabbath Experiment*, 34.

21. On the love of God that involves our mind and thinking, see chapter 1.

22. Muthiah, *The Sabbath Experiment*, 34.

23. Muthiah, *The Sabbath Experiment*, 39.

Chapter 12

The Virtuous Identity

But now, thus says the LORD, *who created you,*
O Jacob, and He who formed you, O Israel:

"Fear not, for I have redeemed you; I have called you
by your name; you are Mine."

—Isaiah 43:1

Through the pages of this book, we have explored a variety of Christian virtues and their corresponding habits: virtuous thinking, faithfulness, loving kindness, courage, patience, humility, contentment, gratitude, prayer, hope in suffering, digital detox, and rest.

These simple habits, when consistently practiced, will enrich our lives, bless others, and bring glory to God. However, when pursuing virtue, we must be careful not to focus only on isolated behaviors. By focusing on isolated behaviors, we are easily tempted to define who we are by what we *do*. We often boast about those areas in which we excel and are successful. While it's true that *what* we do is important, *why* we do it is even more important. Our deepest spiritual identity is not derived from what we do but from who we are and to whom we ultimately belong. Only as we realize who we are, will we be able to live virtuously.

In this chapter, we are going to examine some unique biblical beliefs and scriptural truths that can help us to form a comprehensive virtuous identity. In John 8, Jesus said that the things we believe have the potential to liberate us: "If you abide in My word, you are My disciples indeed. And you shall know the truth, and the truth shall make you free" (John 8:31, 32). With this in mind, let's explore a few of the truths of Scripture that can shape our identities and bring us freedom.

Virtuous believers are aware of God's deep love

The bedrock of our Christian identity is the fact that we are infinitely loved by the God who created and redeemed us. Jesus loved us while we were still His enemies (Romans 5:8, 10). Without His tender love, we wouldn't experience His blessings each day or have any hope of life beyond this painful world. We wouldn't realize our need for forgiveness or have any desire to become more like Jesus. It is only God's deep and persistent love that leads to our conversion—one of the most amazing miracles in the universe. It is only through His love and grace that we are called children of God and heirs of salvation.

Jesus' love creates an identity and value in us that nothing else can ever achieve. The culture we live in constantly tempts us to define our value by competing with others, pushing ourselves to the max, and proving ourselves to be worthy of acceptance and love. But God's love is unconditional and unmerited. His love is not a response to what we have done, but simply the reality of who He is (1 John 4:8). We can never earn God's love or forgiveness but can only accept it in childlike faith. This living faith fills our hearts with hope and gratitude. As God's beloved children, we can know that we are saved through the eternal life that is offered to us through Jesus Christ alone (1 John 5:10–13). What He has done for us enables us to respond in faith to His initiative.

The next chapter will dive deeper into the beautiful truth of Christ's righteousness, but I hope that you have sensed His heartwarming love in every chapter of this book. Of course, it's impossible for any book to exhaust the theme of God's love. As one of my favorite authors has aptly stated:

Tongue cannot utter it; pen cannot portray it. You may meditate upon it every day of your life; you may search the Scriptures diligently in order to understand it; you may summon every power and capability that God has given you, in the endeavor to comprehend the love and compassion of the heavenly Father; and yet there is an infinity beyond. You may study that love for ages; yet you can never fully comprehend the length and the breadth, the depth and the height, of the love of God in giving His Son to die for the world. Eternity itself can never fully reveal it. Yet as we study the Bible and meditate upon the life of Christ and the plan of redemption, these great themes will open to our understanding more and more.[1]

This leads us to the importance of the Word of God for our spiritual identity.

Virtuous leaders are guided by God's deep love

Love requires consistent communication. This is why God speaks to us through His written Word. Love also requires mindful attention to what is communicated. The Bible makes several astounding claims about its origin and its potential to impact our lives. Speaking to a young believer, Paul wrote, "From childhood you have been acquainted with the sacred writings, which are able to make you wise for salvation through faith in Christ Jesus. All Scripture is breathed out by God and profitable for teaching, for reproof, for correction, and for training in righteousness, that the man of God may be complete, equipped for every good work" (2 Timothy 3:15–17, ESV).

The Bible is a *powerful* book. What other book can make a person "wise for salvation"? What other book comes from the very breath of God? What other book can work in countless ways to help *complete* us as human beings, empowering us to live virtuously?

When Jesus was tempted in the wilderness, He taught an important lesson about the relationship we should have with God's Word. Responding to Satan's temptation to turn stones into bread, Jesus said, "It is written, 'Man shall not live by bread alone, but by every word that proceeds from the mouth of God' " (Matthew 4:4).

Jesus' identity was rooted in God's Word. He *lived* by God's Word, letting it shape His mind, heart, actions, and entire life. Heaven invites us to have this same experience with Scripture.

Those who have experienced Christ's transforming love will have the desire to *live by God's Word.* They will find wisdom and joy through the stories and songs, the promises and prophecies, the inspiration and instruction of Scripture.

If we believe that God is love and that He delights to give us the very best (Psalm 84:11), we will be attentive to His commands and His will. This attentiveness will not be selective but will include our willing observance of all of God's Ten Commandments (Exodus 20), as well as the rest of the instruction of Scripture.

But let us be mindful that obedience is never the path to salvation but is rather the joyful heart response of those who have been saved by faith through Jesus Christ. God's commandments are the shoes in which our love for God walks and finds its faithful expression. As the apostle Paul so eloquently stated, "Love is the fulfillment of the law" (Romans 13:10).

Virtuous believers live a lifestyle of *shalom*

The Hebrew language contains a beautiful concept called *shalom.* This word is translated into the English word *peace,* which is a partial but incomplete definition. *Shalom,* in a broader sense, means "completeness, soundness, welfare, peace."[2] *Shalom* refers to the beautiful state of living in harmony with the Creator God and all of His creation. It means living in peaceful reconciliation with God and, as far as it depends on us, to live peaceably with all (Romans 12:18).

If we have truly experienced in our own lives the amazing peace that grows out of God's forgiveness, we will be eager to foster peace, grant forgiveness, and work for reconciliation with others. As we follow the example of Jesus to solve conflicts constructively[3] and nonviolently,[4] Christ's love will become more visible in our lives, and we will experience the blessing of *shalom*.

The gift of the Sabbath can also help us experience *shalom*. The Sabbath reminds us of paradise—of a time when there was complete harmony and peace between God, nature, and humanity. The Sabbath reveals to us that the fellowship with our Creator God is more important for our identity than any work we perform. Before Adam and Eve were able to accomplish any work, they spent time with God on the first Sabbath of Creation week. Out of this holy time with God, everything we do gains its significance. But the Sabbath also points forward to the future when we will experience Sabbath rest in God's new earth (Hebrews 4:1–6).

While many Christians have been misled into thinking the fourth commandment is no longer valid, or that the Sabbath has been changed, I believe the Holy Spirit is working to reveal the truth of the Sabbath, so that virtuous believers everywhere can experience the blessing of Sabbath rest as God intends (Exodus 20:8–11). The Sabbath leads us to set our daily work priorities straight. It reminds us that no matter how diligent and industrious we are, our work will always remain incomplete. Thus, the Sabbath reminds us that we ultimately live by God's grace alone, and find completeness in Him.

Sabbath observance visibly demonstrates our love and faithfulness to our Creator, as a sign that we belong to the only true God. According to Bible prophecy, the Sabbath will play an important role in the final events of earth's history when God's character is contested, and our loyalty to God is challenged.[5]

Virtuous believers have a special understanding of time
While the Sabbath is a gift in time that helps us live virtuously in

our daily lives, God also graciously gives us an understanding of time that helps to prepare us for the long-term future. In His great love, He reveals future events to His children.

> For I am God, and there is no other;
> I am God, and there is none like Me,
> Declaring the end from the beginning,
> And from ancient times things that are not yet done
>   (Isaiah 46:9, 10).

Prophecy increases our confidence in Scripture and in God's ability to accomplish exactly what He says He will do at exactly the right time.

The Bible predicts that the second coming of Christ is near and gives us practical instruction on how to prepare for His coming. In particular, the prophecies of Daniel and Revelation provide us with a unique perspective of world history and a clearer understanding of the times in which we live. In these prophecies, God grants us a glimpse into the great controversy between good and evil. Here, we are told how history will unfold, especially as it relates to the salvation of God's end-time people.

This prophetic view of time can add rich meaning to our lives and help us to prioritize and prepare for the future. Bible prophecy always has Jesus Christ at its center. It is not motivated by sensationalism or conspiracy. Rather, it inspires us to live virtuously as we urgently share with others that Christ's second coming is close at hand (Revelation 14:6; Matthew 28:19).

There is much misinformation and misinterpretation of Bible prophecy in our world today, but the Bible provides clarity and gives its own guidelines for proper interpretation. If you would like to study Bible prophecy in further depth, please see the resources recommended at the end of the chapter.[6] The Bible promises a special blessing to virtuous believers who study end-time prophecy: "Blessed is he who reads and those who hear the words of this prophecy, and keep those things which are written in it; for the time is near" (Revelation 1:3).

Virtuous believers are conscientious stewards

An awareness of the times we live in and of Christ's deep love for humanity will inspire us to be good stewards of the resources God has given us: our time, money, health, talents, relationships, and so on. Good stewardship means carefully managing our time in ways that promote our own growth, as well as the growth of others. This includes taking time for Bible study, prayer, Christian fellowship, witnessing, and rest.

Good stewardship also leads us to avoid wasteful and extravagant habits, choosing instead to live balanced lives of generosity. We are invited to joyfully return our tithes and offerings to the Giver of all good gifts (Malachi 3:8–11). This practice gives us an opportunity to become more like God, who generously and liberally gives every good thing to us (James 1:17). We can abstain from pomp and showiness in possessions, dress, and adornment, choosing instead to reflect God's love through modesty, simplicity, and generosity.

Good stewardship also includes treating our bodies as temples of the Holy Spirit (1 Corinthians 6:19). Our physical health significantly impacts our spiritual well-being and our ability to serve others. We can honor God by conscientiously refraining from all substances and habits that damage health, while actively investing in habits that promote health: nutrition, physical activity, adequate sleep, an attitude of gratefulness, and so on. In the words of the apostle Paul, "Whether you eat or drink, or whatever you do, do all to the glory of God" (1 Corinthians 10:31).

Virtuous believers help those in need

God's children are passionate about helping those in need, irrespective of religious background, gender, socioeconomic status, race, or ethnicity. During His earthly ministry, Jesus spent significant time healing the sick, helping the poor, encouraging those who were sad, and relieving countless types of suffering. The love of Christ compels us to follow His example by ministering to others in practical ways (2 Corinthians 5:14).

Virtuous believers are filled with hope

God's children are propelled by their hope in His goodness and in the soon coming of Jesus. According to Scripture, this beautiful hope inspires virtuous living, "Beloved, now we are children of God; and it has not yet been revealed what we shall be, but we know that when He is revealed, we shall be like Him, for we shall see Him as He is. And everyone who has this hope in Him purifies himself, just as He is pure" (1 John 3:2, 3). In this process of purification, virtuous believers are eager to overcome the power of sin through the "blood of the Lamb" (Revelation 12:11). As we preach and share "the everlasting gospel" (Revelation 14:6), we can demonstrate that we are a people of hope.

Because Jesus was resurrected bodily from the dead, we have the hope of resurrection. All those who die while trusting Jesus Christ will rest in their graves until He comes again: "For the Lord Himself will descend from heaven with a shout, with the voice of an archangel, and with the trumpet of God. And the dead in Christ will rise first. Then we who are alive and remain shall be caught up together with them in the clouds to meet the Lord in the air. And thus we shall always be with the Lord" (1 Thessalonians 4:16, 17).

Even though we don't know the exact time of Christ's return, we can live lives of joyful expectancy and hope—ready to meet Him when He comes. No matter what we face on this earth, we can look forward to the day when God will wipe every tear from our eyes: "There shall be no more death, nor sorrow, nor crying. There shall be no more pain, for the former things have passed away" (Revelation 21:4).

The hope of the Christian is ultimately grounded in Christ's great love for us. This love remains the starting point, the center, and the *telos*[7] of Christian identity. "Not to us, O LORD, not to us, but to Your name give glory, because of Your lovingkindness, because of Your truth" (Psalm 115:1, NASB).

Reflection questions:
1. Why is God's love the most important aspect of Christian identity?
2. What was God's motivation in giving us Scripture?
3. How can the Sabbath help promote a lifestyle of *shalom*?
4. How might you benefit from further study of prophecy?
5. How can stewardship and service enrich our lives?
6. How are you (or how could you be) actively involved in helping others in need?

---

1. Ellen G. White, *Testimonies for the Church* (Mountain View, CA: Pacific Press®, 1948), 5:740.

2. Francis Brown, Samuel Rolles Driver, and Charles Augustus Briggs, *Enhanced Brown-Driver-Briggs Hebrew and English Lexicon* (Oxford: Clarendon Press, 1977), 1022.

3. Matthew 18:15–17 provides a template for constructive conflict resolution. An excellent book on this topic is David Burns, *Feeling Good Together: The Secret of Making Troubled Relationships Work* (New York: Broadway Books, 2008).

4. For a penetrating analysis of the nonviolent way of Christ and the early Christian church and the Adventist perspective on war and military service, see the contributions in Frank M. Hasel, Barna Magyarosi, and Stefan Höschele, eds., *Adventist and Military Service: Biblical, Historical, and Ethical Perspectives* (Madrid: Editorial Safeliz, 2019).

5. If you want to study biblical prophecy in greater depth, I recommend Mark Finley's "Unsealing Daniel's Mysteries" series, which can be found on YouTube and also as online Bible study guides, or David Asscherick's "Discover Prophecy" series, which can be purchased as a set or watched on YouTube.

6. I recommend Pastor Mark Finley's "Unsealing Daniel's Mysteries" series, which can be found on YouTube and also as online Bible study guides, or David Asscherick's "Discover Prophecy" series, which can be purchased as a set or watched on YouTube. I also recommend

Clifford Goldstein's classic book *1844 Made Simple* (Nampa, ID: Pacific Press®, 1998). See also www.1844madesimple.org.

7. *Telos* is the Greek word used in the New Testament to describe the goal and fulfillment of something.

Chapter 13

The Virtue of Jesus

Ecce homo—Behold the Man!
> —John 19:5, Latin Vulgate Translation

Behold the Man! Perhaps these words describe it all. When it comes to exemplifying virtues, there is no better person to behold than Jesus. He is the one-and-only human being who has truly lived virtuously. Through His radically generous life and infinitely sacrificial death, Jesus Christ displayed the most beautiful love the universe has ever seen.

As fallen human beings, we often miss the mark of virtuous living and loving. Although we would like to believe we're capable of living righteously if we try hard enough, the truth is that we must have a power working outside of ourselves to produce the virtues we are incapable of producing.

While humanistic philosophy teaches that we can make ourselves more virtuous through our own efforts, the gospel contradicts this theory: "Can the Ethiopian change his skin or the leopard its spots? Then may you also do good who are accustomed to do evil" (Jeremiah 13:23).

God knows that as human beings, we have a tendency to feel more virtuous than we actually are. If we fall into this trap, we will lose our ability to view ourselves and others objectively and will also forget our dependence on Christ. Self-righteousness inevitably damages our relationships with God, others, and ourselves.

Jesus knew that people who felt too virtuous were in danger of missing the entire point of the gospel. That is why He told the following story:

> Two men went up to the temple to pray, one a Pharisee and the other a tax collector. The Pharisee stood and prayed thus with himself, "God, I thank You that I am not like other men—extortioners, unjust, adulterers, or even as this tax collector. I fast twice a week; I give tithes of all that I possess." And the tax collector, standing afar off, would not so much as raise his eyes to heaven, but beat his breast, saying, "God, be merciful to me a sinner!" I tell you, this man went down to his house justified rather than the other; for everyone who exalts himself will be humbled, and he who humbles himself will be exalted (Luke 18:9–14).

The Pharisees found their sense of security by comparing themselves with others in order to feel morally superior. This is a trap that destroys Christian virtue and erodes genuine faith. We must constantly remember the *actual* standard by which God judges human beings. He does not compare our moral performance with other people—but rather, compares us to His perfect law of love.

Scripture makes it clear that all of us have broken God's law: "Now we know that whatever the law says, it says to those who are under the law, that every mouth may be stopped, and all the world may become guilty before God. . . . For all have sinned and fall short of the glory of God" (Romans 3:19, 23).[1]

Regardless of how virtuous we wish we were, each one of us has a history of *past sin* and a strong pull toward *present sin*. Sin goes beyond mere behavior, reaching deep into our thoughts and motives. But our sinfulness does not scare Jesus away. No matter how dark our past may be, with Jesus, there is a bright future ahead. When questioned about why He spent so much time with sinners, Jesus said, "Those who are well have no need of a physician, but those who are sick. I have not come to call the righteous, but sinners, to repentance" (Luke 5:31, 32).

Jesus is the Great Physician, working to heal and restore us from the damaging effects of sin. In this chapter, I will explore two ways in which He accomplishes this healing:

- By being our virtue
- By empowering us with His virtue through the Holy Spirit

Jesus is our virtue

According to Scripture, God's law requires a perfect record of virtuous living. Because this is the case, we are easily tempted to try to earn, or "merit," God's favor through our works. But creature merit (righteousness coming from a human being) is not just difficult to obtain—it is absolutely impossible. One insightful Christian writer has aptly stated,

> If you would gather together everything that is good and holy and noble and lovely in man and then present the subject to the angels of God as acting a part in the salvation of the human soul or in merit, the proposition would be rejected as treason. . . .
> . . . The idea of doing anything to merit the grace of pardon is fallacy from beginning to end.[2]

Martin Luther, the famous Protestant Reformer, learned this lesson the hard way. Taught from his youth that good deeds could merit God's favor, this young monk worked tirelessly to make himself virtuous. Nevertheless, the harder he worked, the less peace he found. No matter how much he fasted, prayed, and devoted himself to God's work, he was still terrified by a haunting sense of his own sinfulness. Then one day, God revealed the beauty of the gospel to this troubled young man. While climbing the Roman *Scala Sancta*[3] staircase on his knees (an act of penance believed to absolve sin), Martin Luther received a strong impression from the Holy Spirit. The words of Romans 1:17 were indelibly imprinted on his mind, "The just shall live by faith." This was the turning point in his experience. Martin Luther stood up, left the staircase, and began his life-changing work of sharing the message of righteousness by faith. Martin Luther had discovered that *Jesus was his virtue.*

The word *virtue* can be used in a few different ways. It is most commonly used to describe a moral behavior or quality of character (i.e., the virtue of humility). But the word can also be used to explain *a reason for something* (e.g., by virtue of the fact that Christ was always humble, and by virtue of the fact that His righteousness has been accounted to me, God treats me as if *I* have always been humble). The implications of Christ's righteousness are astounding:

- By virtue of the fact that Jesus was always grateful, God credits this virtue to me, even though so many times I have been discontent.
- By virtue of the fact that Jesus was always patient, God views my record through this lens, despite my history of impatience.
- By virtue of the fact that Jesus perfectly fulfilled the law, God treats me as if I'd never disobeyed, even though I have failed countless times.

The beautiful news of the gospel is that Jesus is not only our *example* of Christian virtue, but He *is* also our virtue. According to the apostle Paul, Jesus "became for us wisdom from God—and righteousness and sanctification and redemption" (1 Corinthians 1:30). Jesus became our virtue.

What a sweet relief to know that "there is virtue in the blood of Christ."[4] As you turn away from those things that can never truly satisfy your longings and put your faith in His sacrifice, "the righteousness of Christ will be revealed as your righteousness, *the virtue of Christ as your virtue.*"[5]

With this in mind, let us take a brief look at the life of Christ, gratefully realizing that every virtue He practiced was practiced on our behalf. As our Substitute and Savior, Jesus' entire life was a manifestation of loving virtue.

Christ's virtuous life

Jesus was a *virtuous thinker.* He loved God with all His heart *and* all His mind (Matthew 22:37). Jesus was *friendly.* His eyes radiated a warmth that attracted even little children (Matthew 19:14). Jesus was *kind* (Titus 3:4). "He bowed with tenderest regard to every member of the family of God"[6]

Jesus was *accepting* (John 4:7–30). He loved those who were despised by society. Jesus was *compassionate.* His heart was touched by people's infirmities (Mark 10:46–52; John 5:2–17; Matthew 9:36). Jesus was *merciful.* He offered grace and power to those trapped in sin and shame (John 8:1–11). Jesus was *encouraging.* He spoke hope to the sorrowing and comforted those in grief (Mark 5:22–43; Luke 8:41–56).

Jesus was *patient.* He did not give up on those who were slow to believe (Luke 24:15–32). Jesus was *gentle.* "He exercised the greatest tact and thoughtful, kind attention in His relationships with the people."[7]

Jesus was *courageous.* He did not allow fear or doubt to divert Him from His mission but maintained an authority that the religious leaders of His day did not possess (Mark 1:22; Luke 4:32). Jesus was *honest.* He spoke liberating truths that set people free (John 8:32).

Jesus was *inclusive.* He showed concern not only for the marginalized of society but also for the rich and influential (Luke 19:2–10). Jesus was *empowering.* He entrusted His important mission to a motley crew of fishermen and tax collectors. Jesus was *tenderhearted.* He treated women with respect even when culture did not value them. Jesus was *meek.* He did not seek fame nor did He promote Himself (John 4:2).

Jesus was *obedient.* As a child, He voluntarily submitted to His godly parents (Luke 2:22, 42–52). Jesus was *faithful.* He always obeyed God's will and His Word (John 6:38; Matthew 4:4). Jesus was *grateful.* He willingly accepted the life God had given Him, even though He experienced poverty and had "no place even to lay his head" (Luke 9:58, NLT).

Jesus was a *prayer warrior.* He often rose early in the morning to pray, and earnestly prayed for those who were causing Him pain (Mark 1:35; Luke 23:34). Jesus was a *good steward* of His time. He avoided distractions in order to accomplish His mission (John 17:4). Jesus *practiced rest.* He observed the Sabbath and consistently rested in the Father's love and care (Luke 4:16; Mark 6:30–32).

Jesus was *humble.* "Though he was God, he did not think of equality with God as something to cling to. Instead, he gave up his divine privileges; he took the humble position of a slave and was born as a human being. When he appeared in human form, he humbled himself in obedience to God and died a criminal's death on a cross" (Philippians 2:6–8, NLT).

Jesus was a *peacemaker.* He did not retaliate when mocked and abused (Luke 23:39–41; 6:28) but had the strength to forgive those who mistreated him.[8] Jesus was *virtuous.* "Virtue—the healing power of love—went out from Him to the sick and distressed."[9] Jesus was, is, and always will be *love.* His life, death, and resurrection revealed a quality of love the world had never seen before—love stronger than all the powers of sin and death.

It is impossible to express the beauty of Christ's virtues fully.[10] That is why the apostle John closed his Gospel account with the following words: "And there are also many other things that Jesus did, which if they were written one by one, I suppose that even the world itself could not contain the books that would be written" (John 21:25).

As we ponder the life and love of Jesus, we will be filled with a sense of awe.[11] Our hearts will be warmed with the good news of the gospel, the good news that all of Christ's virtues, all of *His* righteousness, and all of *His* acceptance with the Father have been freely extended to us through the gift of salvation. *Jesus is our virtue.*

Jesus empowers us with virtue

The forgiveness of Christ is sweet, but the good news does not stop there. In addition to forgiveness, we need restoration and also renewal. In addition to pardon, we need strength to live the virtuous lives we were designed to live. Jesus wants us to live in harmony with the principles of love.

We all have an intense desire to be valued and loved. This longing is deep and constant: "What a person desires is unfailing love" (Proverbs 19:22, NIV). Nothing on earth impacts our well-being and happiness more than the quality of our interpersonal relationships. The capacity to know and to be known, to love and to be loved, lies at the very core of human identity.[12] We were created in the image of Love, by Love, and for Love.

Furthermore, because He created us this way, God's deepest desire is to provide us with both the love we need to receive *and* the love we need to give. Christ reveals His rich love toward us in countless ways, and also places people in our lives for us to love (and to be loved by). In order to protect these relationships, we need the graces of Christian virtue. Virtues cause relationships to flourish, leading the way to the richest and most satisfying connections possible.[13]

At the end of the day, virtuous living is all about fulfilling the two greatest commandments, which according to Jesus are "Love the LORD your God with all your heart, and with all your soul, and with all your mind. . . . Love your neighbor as yourself" (Matthew 22:37–39).

Jesus knows that we cannot live virtuously or love adequately on our own. That is why He offers us His *living virtue.* The Bible promises that those who put their trust in Christ receive the gift of the Holy Spirit (Ephesians 1:13). God is eager to give this gift to those who ask Him (Luke 11:13). As we meditate on God's love and His Word, trusting Him as our Righteousness, the Holy Spirit works to bring Christ's active virtues into our lives. This beautiful mystery is what the apostle Paul referred to as "Christ in you, the hope of glory" (Colossians 1:27). In the words of Ellen White, "The Holy Spirit is the breath of spiritual life in the soul. The impartation of the Spirit is the impartation of the life of Christ. It imbues the receiver with the attributes of Christ."[14]

What is our role in this beautiful exchange? To abide in Christ.

God desires to manifest through you the holiness, the benevolence, the compassion, of His own character. Yet the Saviour does not bid the disciples labor to bear fruit. He tells them to abide in Him. "If ye abide in Me," He says, "and My words abide in you, ye shall ask what ye will, and it shall be done unto you." It is through the word that Christ abides in His followers. This is the same vital union that is represented by eating His flesh and drinking His blood. The words of Christ are spirit and life. Receiving them, you receive the life of the Vine. You live "by every word that proceedeth out of the mouth of God." Matthew 4:4. The life of Christ in you produces the same fruits as in Him. Living in Christ, adhering to Christ, supported by Christ, drawing nourishment from Christ, you bear fruit after the similitude of Christ.[15]

My wish for you

Perhaps the most beautiful description of Christian virtue is found in these famous words of the apostle Paul:

If I speak in the tongues of men or of angels, but do not have love, I am only a resounding gong or a clanging cymbal. If I have the gift of prophecy and can fathom all mysteries and all knowledge, and if I have a faith that can move mountains, but do not have love, I am nothing. If I give all I possess to the poor and give over my body to hardship that I may boast, but do not have love, I gain nothing.

Love is patient, love is kind. It does not envy, it does not boast, it is not proud. It does not dishonor others, it is not self-seeking, it is not easily angered, it keeps no record of wrongs. Love does not delight in evil but rejoices with the truth. It always protects, always trusts, always hopes, always perseveres.

Love never fails (1 Corinthians 13:1–8, NIV).

We have come to the end of our exploration of Christian virtue. My hope and prayer is that the pages of this book have warmed your heart with the love of Christ and inspired you to become more like Him through the power of His virtue working in your life. The rewards of Christian virtue are priceless—worth exceedingly more than anything their pursuit may cost, because love never fails.

Reflection questions

1. What aspect of Jesus' character is most attractive and appealing to you? Why?
2. Read 1 Corinthians 13:4–7. Are there any virtues here that might improve your current relationships?
3. What role does the Holy Spirit play in virtuous living?
4. In what ways are you tempted toward self-righteousness?
5. How does it feel to know that Jesus is your Virtue?

1. See also Romans 3:10–12; Isaiah 53:6.

2. Ellen G. White, *Faith and Works* (Nashville, TN: Southern Publishing Association, 1979), 24.

3. According to Catholic tradition, these "holy stairs" are the stairs Jesus ascended to meet with Pilate prior to His crucifixion. It has been claimed that these stairs were transported from Jerusalem to Rome. The Roman Catholic Church has offered various indulgences to people for climbing the staircase on their knees. In the time of Martin Luther, it was believed that this act could release a soul from purgatory.

4. Ellen G. White, Letter 206, July 14, 1908, par. 13.

5. Ellen G. White, *Selected Messages*, bk. 1 (Washington, D.C.: Review and Herald®, 1958), 330; emphasis added. The author goes on to say: "You will then understand that justification will come alone through faith in Christ; for in Jesus is revealed the perfection of the character of God; in His life is manifested the outworking of the principles of holiness. Through the atoning blood of Christ the sinner is set free from bondage and condemnation; through the perfection of the sinless Substitute and Surety, he may run in the race of humble obedience to all God's commandments. Without Christ he is under the condemnation of the law, always a sinner, but through faith in Christ he is made just before God" (330).

6. Ellen G. White, *The Desire of Ages* (Mountain View, CA: Pacific Press®, 1940), 353.

7. Ellen G. White, *Steps to Christ* (Mountain View, CA: Pacific Press®, 1956), 12.

8. For an account of the peaceful way of Jesus and the early church that refused to use weapons and did not join the military, see the discussion in Frank M. Hasel, Barna Magyarosi, and Stefan Höschele, eds., *Adventists and Military Service: Biblical, Historical, and Ethical Perspectives* (Madrid: Editorial Safeliz, 2019).

9. White, *The Desire of Ages*, 92. See also Luke 8:46.

10. If you want to explore the beauty of Christ's interactions with people, read the Gospels! You may also enjoy the following books: Ken Gire, *Intimate Moments With the Savior: Learning to Love* (Grand Rapids, MI: Zondervan, 1989); Roberto Badenas, *Decisive Encounters* (Nampa, ID: Pacific Press®, 2019), and the best-selling book and classic by Ellen G. White, *The Desire of Ages*.

11. Cf. Paul David Tripp, *Awe: Why It Matters for Everything We Think, Say, and Do* (Wheaton, IL: Crossway, 2015).

12. Cf. Gregory E. Ganssle, *Our Deepest Desires: How the Christian Story Fulfills Human Aspirations* (Downers Grove, IL: InterVarsity Press, 2017), 35.

13. Cf. Ganssle, *Our Deepest Desires*, 67.

14. White, *The Desire of Ages*, 805.

15. White, *The Desire of Ages*, 677.